Janet captures the Mind Body & Spirit connection of MONEY through a soulful journey, to help you understand the energy and emotions around abundance. Right from the first chapter, Money Mirror, she explains the inner workings of prosperity and how this is reflected in the outer world the reverse of what we are often taught. Janet helps you find your TRUTH to transform your relationship(s) with money and with vulnerability and courage, she speaks to the heart, from her heart, as though she is guiding and walking alongside you.

Karie Cassell,
#1 Bestselling Author of The Domino Diet: How to Heal You from the Inside Out

A powerful guide to self-discovery, empowerment and transforming your story. Through personal anecdotes and reflective prompts, the author encourages readers to embrace authenticity and honesty in their lives. By reframing their stories, readers can uncover opportunities for growth and abundance. The book delves into the connection between self-worth and abundance, inspiring courage to explore one's true identity and claim worthiness in all aspects of life. With a focus on introspection and self-inquiry, readers are prompted to examine their beliefs about themselves and their reality. The author sheds light on the profound impact of self-perception on relationships and manifestations, emphasizing the importance of nurturing a positive relationship with oneself. This book offers invaluable insights and practical tools for those seeking personal transformation from the inside out.

Andrea Salway, BEd, MA in Counselling Psychology

I just finished reading Heal Your Money, Heal Your Life by Janet Kendrick. For years I didn't understand that money was energy, or my money was a reflection of my life and my relationship with money. It took me years to heal my own relationship with money and reading this great book, it occurs to me if I could have discovered this book years ago, I would have skipped so many of my own money challenges. This book is a must read if you too have a challenging relationship with money.

Corey Poirier, 5x TEDx Speaker, Wall Street Journal /
USA Today Bestselling Author, bLU Talks Founder

Janet Kendrick's 'Heal Your Money, Heal Your Life' isn't just a book; it's a transformative journey into the depths of our financial and personal landscapes. With warmth and wisdom, Janet introduces readers to the fascinating concept of money archetypes, offering a profound exploration of how these hidden influences shape our financial choices. Through heartfelt storytelling and practical exercises, she guides readers on a path of self-discovery, encouraging them to trust their intuition and dive deeper into the layers of their soul for true healing. More than a mere guidebook, this work is an odyssey of resilience and empowerment, providing both insights and tools to navigate the complexities of our financial lives with grace. Ultimately, Janet reveals that our relationship with money is a reflection of our inner selves and our connections with others, offering a roadmap to abundance and fulfillment that transcends the realm of finance.

Candace McKim,
Intuitive Manifestation Coach,
#1 International Bestselling Author and TEDx Speaker
https://www.candacemckim.com/

Janet takes you through a journey of personal and intimate experiences, past stories, and events that have strengthened her belief that the 'key to happiness is to live your truth.' She provides excellent tools and examples to help the reader align their body, spirit and soul and achieve freedom in all aspects of their life. This is a book written about mastering money for women, but it will also benefit and empower any man!

Alex Cardenas,
Leadership Performance Coach

Heal Your Money, Heal Your Life is a compassionate guide for women to gain both competence and confidence with their finances. Janet Kendrick explains that money is a tool that teaches us where we are leaking energy and gives us tangible ways to take back our power. She compassionately reminds us that building a net worth is important, however aligning with our "enlightened net worth" is the most empowering thing we can do!

**Christine M Luken,
author of Financial Dignity After Divorce &
host of the Money is Emotional podcast**

Janet's raw vulnerability and insightful storytelling guide us to introspect using money as a reflective tool. Join her on a spiritual journey through diverse practices, feeling as if you're right there with her. This book offers profound questions to deepen your self-awareness and money relationship. Read this book to dive into the transformative portal of money and self-discovery.

**Rosalyn Fung,
Transformational Leadership Business Coach & Spiritual Guide**

I wish this insightful, inspirational, and motivational book had been required reading in my high school years fifty years ago! It would have totally changed the trajectory of my life, my relationships, and my business ventures!

'Heal Your Money, Heal Your Life' is a true LIFE-CHANGER! It is helping me bring to fruition my dreams and goals of being a Kingdom philanthropist as I overcome my fears. Much pain and suffering in The School of Hard Knocks could be avoided if this book was required reading by every high school student!

Ulrike Wohlfarth Levins

HEAL YOUR MONEY
HEAL YOUR LIFE
A Healing Guide for Freedom Seekers

Janet Kendrick

Heal Your Money Heal Your Life
A Healing Guide for Freedom Seekers
Janet Kendrick

Published by Prosperous Woman Coaching, Grande Prairie, Alberta, Canada
Copyright ©2024 Janet Kendrick
All rights reserved.

No part of this publication may be reproduced, stored in a retrieval system, or transmitted in any form or by any means, electronic, mechanical, photocopying, recording, scanning, or otherwise, except as permitted under Section 107 or 108 of the 1976 United States Copyright Act, without the prior written permission of the Publisher. Requests to the Publisher for permission should be addressed to Permissions Department, Prosperous Woman Coaching, prosperous4women@gmail.com

Limit of Liability/Disclaimer of Warranty: While the publisher and author have used their best efforts in preparing this book, they make no representations or warranties with respect to the accuracy or completeness of the contents of this book and specifically disclaim any implied warranties of merchantability or fitness for a particular purpose. No warranty may be created or extended by sales representatives or written sales materials. The advice and strategies contained herein may not be suitable for your situation. You should consult with a professional where appropriate. Neither the publisher nor author shall be liable for any loss of profit or any other commercial damages, including but not limited to special, incidental, consequential, or other damages.

This is a work of fiction. The story, all names, characters, and incidents portrayed in this literary work are fictitious. No identification with actual persons (living or deceased), places, buildings, and products is intended or should be inferred. Any similarity to actual persons, living or deceased, or actual events, is purely coincidental.

Project Management and Book Design: Davis Creative Publishing, LLC / DavisCreativePublishing.com

Janet Kendrick
Heal Your Money Heal Your Life: A Healing Guide for Freedom Seekers
ISBN: 978-1-0688510-2-5 (paperback)
         978-1-0688510-1-8 (ebook)

SEL016000   SELF-HELP / Personal Growth / Happiness
SEL023000   SELF-HELP / Personal Growth / Self-Esteem
SEL032000   SELF-HELP / Spiritual

2024

ATTENTION CORPORATIONS, UNIVERSITIES, COLLEGES AND PROFESSIONAL ORGANIZATIONS: Quantity discounts are available on bulk purchases of this book for educational, gift purposes, or as premiums for increasing magazine subscriptions or renewals. Special books or book excerpts can also be created to fit specific needs. For information, please contact Prosperous Woman Coaching, prosperous4women@gmail.com, janetkendrick.com

Contents

Preface	1
Introduction	5
Money as a Mirror	9
The Energy of Money	13
Prosperous Woman	19
The Power of Archetypes	25
Changing Your Story	41
Money as a Mirror	45
Life in Fragments	57
The Energy of Our Bodies	69
Live Your Truth	85
Union of Mind, Body, Soul	95
The Energy of Fear	103
The Energy of Love	117
Love that Binds	131
Love Endings	137
Letting Go	151
Whom Was I Serving?	159

Shadow Side of Money	173
Archetypes	177
You are Empathic	195
Returning Home	201
Truth	209
Epilogue	213
About the Author	219
Additional Resources	221

Preface

Perhaps as a child, you didn't receive approval, love, or positive opinions from important people around you. You have a dream that has planted your heart; it is not with vanity or selfishness that you want to serve, so you go deeper to let go of what is holding you back from getting there. You wish to move from living in fear to being more in a place of love, where we can value each other, let go of the judgments and labels, and instead practice more compassion and love for one another. Our truest value is not found in our bank accounts but in the unconditional place from the heart center.

HOW DO WE CONNECT WITH THE HEART?

Yoga came into my life to teach me to slow down and to listen to the whispers of my soul. To release the stuck emotions like shame and guilt from my past experiences, calm and recalibrate a nervous system that once thought abuse, violence, and control was a normal way of living. Teaching me to live more in alignment through embracing the courage required to take a different path, trusting the inner wisdom to be my guide, and always knowing I was never alone. Yoga helped me slow down to experience my natural gifts as a teacher. On the mat, I connected with God and felt the spirit move through me, expressing its will even when I didn't have the strength to do it alone.

I did not understand energy. Yet inside, I knew I needed healing. Healers came into my life as gentle, compassionate guides to look at my inner child's wounds, help me understand why people hurt me and see where others lacked the tools or guidance to do better. I could apply forgiveness, which opened me to receive more love. It's the love from another who could hold space for me to shine the light onto the dark spaces necessary for my inner growth.

I was drawn to horses. At first, I felt fear until I understood how sensitive they were to our energy. In my body, I felt fear, the stiffness and rigidity of my once inflexible body. Horses guided me to listen, to challenge me, and to show me how capable I was of becoming more. Horses taught me how to carry my power and feel the freedom in my body once it was received.

God is my guide, forever present, and most lovingly, he held space for my journey back home to my birthright of love. On May 15, 2005, I accepted Jesus Christ as God's son and that he died for our sins. I did it because I wanted to be close to God more than anything. While I was immature in my understanding of Christ then, my journey would expand me to being more in the spirit of Christ's consciousness as I thrived to be more loving, gentle, and compassionate with myself and others. I respect the lessons he taught and now have a deeper understanding of how the bible offers a pathway to live life more in alignment. It's a story told in love.

After my baptism, I felt an energy or spirit move through me. I was never alone; I would ask questions and receive answers. I would be guided by dreams, my inner knowingness, and during teaching or speaking. I make it a point to ask him to speak through me with complete confidence that the words will come. I invite you to explore your attitudes and beliefs that are blocking your way from receiving this truth and freedom.

The key to happiness is to live your truth. I admit I have some fear about releasing my story. I know the judgments of this world can be harsh. I was reminded recently about a time when I was in grade 9. I returned from lunch and had gotten high when my guidance counselor waved a paper I wrote in my face. I didn't understand at first, then noticed an "A" circled in red ink. He informed me that I had won first place in a contest I had written and submitted for Drug Awareness Week. It was a story I had shared about my struggles as a teenager and why I used marijuana to numb my pain. I didn't want to do it or know what else to do. Telling my truth was painful and healing for me. I share because I care about the struggles that we often inflict upon ourselves and others. After all, we have been imprinted to believe we are something we are not and live a lie. It is up to us to dig deeper subconsciously to rid ourselves of the beliefs that punish us and reimprint ourselves with the lives God intended us to live.

Heaven on earth is a result of the choices that we make. We cannot change the world. However, I believe with all my heart that who we become can positively impact this world.

Introduction

My intention with this book is to provide a self-directed, inspirational journey that will engage healing around the topics of self and money. As you read this book, my wish is that you experience feelings of compassion, love, and understanding for the parts of yourself that want to reconnect.

This book has been written for women who seek independence and freedom, and those who are ready to observe where they are now and are eager to truly envision where they want to be. Such observations and visions require honesty, authenticity, and a disciplined approach to inner work. The content I share is meant to provide support and resources, which is the other purpose for writing this book: to ignite self-inquiry and find answers as you discover your truth. While I've written this book for women, for the few men who are curious about my words, it's a guidebook for you and may provide insights for you and your partner.

I want women to feel the pain of their past behaviors, and their experiences, and then breathe understanding, forgiveness, and love into those wounds. I want the energy of love to work in the shadow parts of themselves so they can break free of the chains forged by patterns and behaviors that prevent them from having a flourishing life. My wish is for you to be able to transform your current philosophy of life from one of scarcity to one of prosperity. I want women to see what is possible, not just for themselves, but for future generations and their partners. I want women who struggle with unhappiness, despair, or depression to know that the struggle will lessen once they embody the truth that they are loved and that we were born enough.

I have provided tools and strategies within this book to help identify and move through fears to evoke images of a brighter future. I want women to understand the power of thoughts and emotions around money and other relationships and let that power mirror who we are. I want women to know they are incredibly capable of designing independent lives, separate from a man or any other person in their lives, and, if they choose, become a more awakened partner who seeks harmony for everyone.

My purpose in life has been to heal and inspire others to do the same. Only when we discover the power that comes from understanding our patterns, behaviors, and energy, will we be able to make the necessary changes to be our highest selves and not be held hostage by our fears or limitations. The basic message is to inspire healing so that women can feel whole and embody love by embracing all parts of themselves, knowing life will provide us with guidance and clues that reveal themselves along the way when we are open enough to receive and understand all of who we are. The more we open ourselves up to the divine, the more we can receive by making conscious right choices. We open by healing the wounds from past experiences, clearing limiting beliefs, and releasing emotions of the past that keep showing up in the present.

I intend to open myself as a vessel, to communicate words from spirit, to evoke healing by sharing my own stories of healing and becoming whole. I believe dreams and our heart's desires can come true and that answers are found in knowing ourselves, expanding self-awareness, developing emotional mastery, and living more consciously in the present.

But enough about what I want. It's time to ask the question:

"What do you want?"

Money as a Mirror

HEAL YOUR MONEY, HEAL YOUR LIFE

This title came to me at 3:00 in the morning. This is the time I usually receive messages from my higher self about an action I am to take or an answer to a question. That early morning, I was not comfortable with the title, but I knew that one day, I would write a book about the lessons our money relationships can teach us about healing ourselves. We all have a money story, imprinted on us when we were younger, witnessing behaviors and patterns of our role models: parents, family, or friends. We were innocent and could not recognize the unconscious ways we imprint the patterns that were part of our early lives, which then became the patterns we acted out later in life. Negative past experiences create money wounds, along with feelings of shame, guilt, or blame that rob us of inner power. Wounds are our unhealed life lessons that will show up in money patterns and behaviors: the ones we hold within ourselves and those that are acted out in relationships.

There are no shortages of money challenges or fears in our lives. It is in facing these that we move through higher levels of success and awaken to higher consciousness levels. When it comes to success, we must question, what does it mean to me to be successful?

For me, success is defined by what matters most to me and whether I am living my truth. *What does it mean to you?*

I have learned that the key to happiness is to live your truth. To live your truth, you must understand and embrace your enlightened net worth, which is to be in the energy of love, joy, abundance, creativity, inspiration, and kindness. Money played a key role in helping me understand more of my truth by getting to the core of who holds the most value and worth.

As a woman, I had three distinct desires: happiness, healthy relationships, and financial freedom. For a woman seeking financial freedom, the ultimate freedom is found within. For me to achieve these three desires, I had to go deeper within myself to heal from past wounds, both in relationships and with money. Our money wounds can make us feel *less than*, or that something is wrong with us. Shame from past behaviors can rob us of experiencing more joy now. On the other hand, money can teach us to wake up and know ourselves on a deeper level, so that we can sort through the noise of the world and recognize the importance of mastering our emotions. We do this by understanding the messages being communicated to us and through mastery of them.

We are always imprinting ourselves. Reliving past experiences can rob us of seeing or experiencing an abundance of opportunities in the present moment. Projecting more worry or fear at the moment creates more of what we don't want in the future.

Rather than worry, get clear about what you want and breathe love and faith into your future desire without too much attachment to how it will work out. I love this verse in the Bible, as it speaks to prayers being fulfilled. *If you remain in me and my words remain in you, ask whatever you wish, and it will be done for you. John 15:7*

When you look into a mirror, what is the reflection you see beyond your facial features? What emotions are evoked when you look deeper? There are truths that money can teach you about yourself and how you can navigate through the self-limiting patterns of your unconscious that rise to your concious mind.

This book is a guide to help you raise your level of wealth consciousness and expand your perceptions by aligning with the abundance already within you.

When you look at money, what emotions are the most predominant? What is the history between you and money or the relationships with others in your life? Do you like what you see or is there something you wish to change? I like to recommend that you become a witness to what is showing up for you and get curious about knowing yourself more intimately.

As you read the words, notice how you feel. Do you recognize what is true for you? Or is it an inherited belief passed to you by another that is no longer in service to who you are or what you want to become? Slip into independent thinking and simply let go of anything that does not resonate with you. If you find yourself resisting and are in denial, know that when we deny parts of ourselves, it is not a recipe for success. It fuels avoidance. I believe raising our level of consciousness means accepting all parts of ourselves — both shadow and light. If we can do that for ourselves, then we can do that for others. Acknowledging the parts of ourselves that we don't like, and shifting from a place of blame, judgment, guilt, or criticism moves us to a place of responsibility. We are each responsible for our mental, emotional, spiritual, physical, and financial well-being. On the wellness wheel of life, when any of these are out of alignment, we may not feel that our lives are in harmony or that we are living to our highest potential.

This is why I've written this book to be a guide for you to live life more in alignment so that you can experience more happiness, healthier relationships, and financial freedom.

Money as a mirror will reveal when you are out of alignment, where you devalue yourself, and your worth. I invite you to lean in and look closely to see the amazing insights money can teach you.

The Energy of Money

Abundance is not something we acquire. It is something we tune into. There is no scarcity of opportunity to make a living at what you love. There is only a scarcity of resolve to make it happen.

—WAYNE DYER

I have not always had a good relationship with money. Honestly, I couldn't figure out why. It puzzled me for years. I've done healing work to achieve a sense of harmony surrounding my mental, emotional physical, and spiritual health. The inner work that I did in my early years had taken me to a place of wholeness, happiness, and true love for myself. The missing piece was in my seeking financial freedom.

I was a guest speaker on a panel of women on the topic of money when a speaker mentioned four words that spoke directly to my soul. *The energy of money.*

That one comment sent me deep inside and I knew I needed to know more. I understood energy. I experienced it when I engaged in healing work that would transform my life from depression and unhappiness to being happy and fulfilled – body and soul. I understood the power energy played in healing my childhood wounds and freeing my soul as I grew to find the love I had been seeking inside myself. I had come to understand what I thought about was what I felt about, which led to the actions I would take in my life. I consciously changed my once unhappy, unhealthy reality towards a joy-filled, healthy life by transforming my negative self-limiting beliefs into loving, kind thoughts. I had seat-of-the-soul moments for change, was to recognize the negative thoughts *at the moment* they arrived and change them into positive ones. Changing my negative thinking about myself into self-love and kindness transformed my life.

What did my thoughts and words have to do with my relationship with money? I immediately started to pay attention to my thoughts and emotions about money. I answered questions about my journey with money which alerted me to a common theme. *There was never enough*. Which also translated to me that *I was not good enough*. This was a deep-rooted belief that was playing out in my reality with money. I noticed feelings of anxiety when I spent money, along with other negative emotions, such as guilt, shame, and judgment. Looking into the mirror, my money truths hit me right in the face. I had money wounds that needed to be healed. As I began to dig deeper, I realized I didn't recognize my true value or my worth. I lacked complete belief in myself. An awareness of these truths started me on the journey to healing myself by looking into my money relationship to see exactly what it was mirroring for me and what I needed to heal. These emotions would lead me on a pathway to higher understanding of myself and the patterns that showed up in my relationships with men and friends in my life. It also revealed to me that I lacked boundaries because, at that time, I did not know the value of what I needed to hold as sacred.

I had the tools to begin and knew what to do; I had already been down this road in my search for happiness, building confidence and self-esteem in my personal life. It was time to observe my negative thoughts about money:

- I never trusted money to be there for me.
- I strived for higher financial goals and never felt like it was enough.
- I judged the level of my success by my bank account balance (never enough).
- I would often spend compulsively, valuing status above financial security.
- The *Common theme…. Never enough.*

Inside of me, this rooted belief of not-enoughness was playing out in my world along with other fears and beliefs. Fears of responsibility. Fear of success/failure. Fear of not being approved of, losing my identity and ones I loved. It was Jung who said *until you make the unconscious conscious, it will direct your life and you will call it fate.*

I had regrets about how I spent money or sold things that were important to me. I would beat myself up repeatedly with judgment, and criticism, too often swimming in my sea of fear, creating more of what I did not want versus what I wanted - which was financial freedom. I did not find freedom in my bank account balance. I could only find freedom by breaking the chains of beliefs, fears, and patterns that prevented me from becoming who I was destined to become: *my best self*. This required accepting all parts of me and choosing what aligned with this inner guidance system that was calling to me. This force that is within ourselves can be unstoppable, depending on your level of determination and resilience. I know that I am not alone in my search as it is the spirit within me that directs the way. The more I ask it and clear myself to receive it, the more power and presence fill my life. My job is to be self-aware and listen, have patience, and trust.

I answered questions about my money story found in the book *The Energy of Money* by Maria Nemeth, Ph.D. How I grew up, what my parents were like, and how that story was playing a role in my life now. I grew up with little money, at times dependent on government systems, with a non-supporting father. I grew up feeling like I was not enough because of what I lacked in my life: love, positive attention, respect, and money. I grew up in a scarcity of love and money which provided an unstable ground for a little girl to feel value or find worth on this big, blue planet. I needed to discover that my value is beyond measure, and I was born enough. So were you.

Money was revealing parts of myself to me that needed healing. It was showing up in multiple ways. I lacked belief in who I was as an individual. My insecurity about who I was as a professional was dragging me down. Emotions triggered by my fears became obvious and I ran towards them, breaking free of my limitations. I slowed life down to practice meditation and yoga daily. I started to receive inspired information and took immediate action by writing it down and sharing it in speeches and workshops. I felt inspired, excited, and knew my purpose as I began to shed my blocks and fears around myself and money. I invested time and money in coaches, mentors, and master-your-money boot camp programs in my search for more.

I took imperfect but inspired action based on the guidance I received. I was creating from a new place inside me, the place where "I am enough." I began to declutter negative emotions and past experiences, and in my dreams, I would arrive at the top of the mountain. I forgave past mistakes and became clearer and freer as I embraced more of my truth and the abundance within me. My inner garden was beginning to flourish in love as I realized that to have a healthy relationship with money, I needed to give it positive, respectful attention and get clear about its purpose in my life. Equally as important, I needed to give myself the same qualities. I practiced gratitude and deep heartfelt joy over my life, rewards, and money. I acted on my savings and other financial goals that were important to me. Taking correct action to move towards the attainment of my goals aligned my future with inner abundance I was seeking: Love.

My inner world began to change, and in the outer world, people who needed my help started arriving . I was invited to be a keynote speaker and was given the honor of being nominated for a Woman of Influence Award. When the city was looking for professionals for their marketing photos, they asked me . New opportunities were revealing themselves every day. The opportunities came as a result of the changes in my foundation. My soul felt fulfilled.

I began teaching people about the meaning of enlightened net worth, and implicitly, how amazing they were as individuals, that they were and will always be their greatest asset, and that they need to love who they are and commit to the importance of self-care. The choice to choose yourself is rarely easy at first. Breaking free of the imprints of unwanted patterns is a battle.

On a deeper level, I realized that true financial freedom is not about growing our net worth. Financial freedom begins when we practice leadership over ourselves and our money management. Financial freedom comes when we feel good about ourselves and money after we've let go of all the blame, guilt, shame, and judgment. Financial freedom arrives when we know our value and worth and place healthy boundaries in place to protect what is sacred within us: sacred strengths, gifts, and talents waiting to be expressed to their fullest potential. Financial Freedom is when each of us knows "I am Enough," regardless of the balance in our bank account. The greater balance in your account may magnify more of who you are. If you are a kind and generous person, you will be more of that, just as if you were the opposite. You are who you are; having more money does not make you better or more important than another. I know now that most people forget who they truly are along the way. They believe through life's experiences and traumas that they are not good enough and they stop loving themselves. I became the embodiment of a prosperous woman with a sustained sense of wellness and harmony in all areas of wellness. It's about working from the inside out.

T. Harv Eker, who wrote the book *Secrets of the Millionaire Mind* quotes:

To change the fruits, we must change the roots.
To change the visible, we must change the invisible.

Prosperous Woman

The word "prosperous" means to expand materially and flourish financially. A definition of prosperous that I resonate with is to expand from within, to flourish in abundance, and to become the essence of love, openness, creativity, and joy. To me, a prosperous woman is expanding, growing in alignment with the highest version of herself. I went from being a shy insecure woman to the woman I am today: open, loving, and confident. I declared this exact affirmation in my twenties on a lake in Tahoe. It created a new imprint, opposite of who I was at that time and as I changed on the inside, my external life changed. The deeper I went, the more my life shifted.

Minding your money relationships provides an opportunity for tremendous growth.

Our emotions around money will teach us how free we really are.

Ask yourself, "What is money?"

Money is nothing without you. It's a coin, plastic, or paper. It's a tool that we use in exchange for our gifts, products, or services. If money is a tool, is it possible that when we are withholding our gifts and talents by being in a career or relationship that feels soul-sucking, that it is about ourselves and not money? Yet we may find ourselves blaming money as the reason we need to stay.

Consider this. Rather than staying out of alignment, get to know ourselves. If we feel worthy, we will say yes to our heart's inner calling. What would it look like if we faced our fears and stepped out with courage and faith in our inner guidance that wants us be in harmony? Who is holding us back, money or ourselves?

Why is then that money can take away our power? Women feel guilty or resentful about asking for or wanting more. Conversations with spouses about why they want to create debt to go into business are difficult. Men feel the pressure of being the main provider and women strive to be equal contributors but may have given years to motherhood rather than a profession. We lack the support to give attention to one another's dreams and goals which can be seen throughout the imbalance of power and emotions in relationship dynamics. Fears or outdated beliefs may prevent individuals or couples from reaching their fullest potential. Can we change, and can we as couples break the chains that hold us to an unfulfilling past? Can we have the courage and faith to face our present with eyes wide open with a common goal to live life more in harmony with one another?

Have you ever been asked or asked yourself the question, "Who do you think you are?" The question itself is telling. It may provide an insight that is full of doubt and insecurity. We hold ourselves back not because of who we think we are, but who we've been taught to think about who we are, or who we can't be.

What I have discovered is who I am is more. I am more capable and powerful than I have yet to fully realize. That power is within me, something that I can access. It is in each of us, and it seeks expression to move through us when we use our unique gifts and talents.

Your talents are not yours to keep hidden. They were given to you so you could be of service in this world. Who are you serving? Money or God.

As a woman who has been through two divorces, I know the risk of being dependent upon someone else for what I feel is my responsibility. It's important to acknowledge that you are responsible for your mental, emotional, spiritual, physical, and financial well-being. This is important: Isn't harmony on earth everyone's responsibility? Can being overly dependent manifest as a way of protecting ourselves or can we learn to become interdependent? In a world where we all have power; may we use it for more good than harm. It is each individual's choice. The thing is, we are all shaped by our own stories and motivations. Another Bible quote may provide an answer, it reads like this:

"You have heard that it was said, love your neighbor, and hate your enemies. But I tell you, love your enemies and pray for those who persecute you. *Matt 5:44*

To me, this allows us an opportunity to place a potential problem in the hands of our higher power. Through prayer we can release what otherwise has a negative hold over us. If we stay in the presence of love, we are sending love in exchange for what might be worrisome and rob us of our power. Love and fear are both powerful forces, along with all of the emotions that reside under each umbrella. We get to choose.

In every opportunity we get to choose to sin or hit the mark; to be in alignment with the truth about who we are and how we live: in love or fear. Who holds authority over you is a fair question to ask? Our emotions can hold clues, and I knew the truth of this line when I heard it, about healthy people *feel.*

Our emotions around money can teach us how free we are.

In my business as a prosperous woman, I felt I was living my purpose by sharing my gifts and wisdom. I have discovered healing modalities and inspired others to do the same. I work with mainly women to help them identify the root of their own limitations. I remind them they too are answering a calling. Their intuition is calling them to discover more about their gifts and talents so they can show up differently in the world. That difference is found in authentic connection.

We often walk around disconnected or negative in our money relationship rather than using it to align with our values or in ways that are positive. Money is a tool that teaches women where they leak energy, but it can be used to take their power back. For a woman seeking financial freedom, the ultimate freedom is found within. Building our net worth is important, however, *aligning with our enlightened net worth is empowering.*

Isn't it also true that most of us are walking around disconnected to ourselves, using or abusing ourselves in ways that are not in alignment. When we begin to awaken to a higher truth about ourselves, this changes. Each of us is enough.

You are enough. You were born with a right to be here. You were born with great value and worth. Awakening to a higher truth is a process that opens you to feeling deserving of a prosperous life. You begin to own your value and embody the truth that you are love. To live with these higher emotions is to be prosperous. This is your place of liberation.

The Power of Archetypes[1]

An archetype is a pattern that connects people of the world across time and culture. It is the original pattern from which copies are made, the beginning or origin of the pattern, model or type.

In a training by Kendall Summerhawk in the spring of 2020, I learned that archetypes teach us about ourselves. Archetypes reveal the power of our patterns. To transform how we think and feel about ourselves, our relationships, and our money, we need to examine our patterns to understand who we are on a deeper level so that we can stand in our truths. For me and others that I worked with, understanding our archetypal language gives us the ability to expand our consciousness and take back our power. Not understanding our patterns can limit our power.

Many of us set intentions–we call them goals–at the beginning of a new year. This is an example of an archetype, the setting of new inten-

---

[1] Have you discovered your sacred money archetype? Go to Heal Your Money, Heal Your Life (www.janetkendrick.com) for more information on archetypes and other tools that you can use to achieve wholeness and align with your best life.

tions, often to be more purposeful in how we create our lives. We may make new commitments to join the gym, quit smoking, eat healthier, or practice more self-care. The statistics tell us that by February we may give up. The reasons lie just beneath the surface. We do not feel deserving or worthy enough. We might not be grounded or feel secure in who we are, which is necessary to keep empowering new choices that will get us where we want to be. Breaking habits or patterns isn't easy, and too often, we keep going it alone, never asking for help or looking deeper at the roots of the problem.

A woman who desires happiness, healthy relationships, and financial freedom must first look within herself. No external resource or person can provide these things because achieving each of them is an *inside job*. However, they can be a mirror by reflecting what we need to see about ourselves and bring our pieces back together.

For half of my life, I prayed for someone to love me, attaching to relationships that did not give me what I needed. The truth was, I did not know what I needed. I had to live half my lifetime doing and being what I didn't like before I began to move towards what I did want. Every new layer of understanding brought me closer to the love I was seeking, and it was my inner guidance that kept highlighting the way to more love. While others mirrored what I needed to see to get clearer, it was my connection with God that brought me closer to what I wanted. I was seeking love, and the answers came from within by trusting and listening to my intuition. I trusted that God would provide, and I followed that guidance. Eventually love enabled me to see that much of what was outside myself was not what was most fulfilling. Peace came in full force when I got down on my knees and prayed to God because I could no longer trust myself. I felt I had made too many changes and was completely stripped down. Too often, I felt the message of Job in the Bible who was in the hands of the enemy. After being in a high place of love, where I didn't think I would ever lose it, I would later then experience life consciously living in fear. I was going against myself by not living in alignment with my gifts or valuing who I was. I allowed something or someone to have power over my life. I became small and limited. The freedom I once felt was stripped away. I wasn't strong enough, yet, as a woman and I needed time to anchor to a new foundation.

When our patterns play out in our world they contain our stories, beliefs, gifts, and talents. Do they also contain insights into what motivates us: is love or an unconscious fear the driver? We make choices all the time, so how can we make more empowered choices versus disempowered choices that keep us trapped in living a life we do not want to create?

Early in my life, I made plenty of disempowered choices which gave me what I did not want in life. Unhappiness and struggle were the result of all my poor choices. Those times when we make disempowered choices, we tend to lean more toward the victim side of ourselves, going into shame, blame, doubt, questioning, and insecurity. When we continually slip into these negative patterns, we enter the place within ourselves that creates inner conflict, the place where life feels like a struggle. We are struggling because we are going against the truth of ourselves, staying trapped in our fearful side rather than rising above it. One day in church I received an answer: when there is a wave of fear, look inward or up, then trust and rise above that wave of fear. When we make an empowered choice, we move inward toward being more connected by exploring the answers within ourselves and moving through the resistance of our fears. Rather than staying limited by this resistance, the remedy is to move through it. It does no good avoiding it.

If I do not know the answer yet, I lean in, asking *the source* who, for me, is God, trusting that I will receive the answer in some way through people, books, dreams, or inner knowing along with synchronicities, and coincidences that show up in life along with my intuition. As I grew in relationship with myself by deepening my connection to source, I looked less to others and more to my inner knowing.

A higher power requires us to tap into different levels of communication to assist us in accessing or expressing from higher parts of ourselves. First, we must access those higher parts within ourselves. Look at our thoughts, the words that come out of our mouths: are they in alignment with our souls? By being in alignment, we can access more of the infinite power of God, and we can use this energy design a life in connection with co-creation. Being in alignment means acting in integrity with what we want in thoughts, emotions, and actions. We can't be too fixed or attached to how we want things to work out. Being inflexible can stop the flow of being inspired or in spirit.

Archetypes are a part of the original universal language and play a role in how people once and still do communicate using signs, symbols, and synchronicities. We also communicate that way when we tap into our intuition, which will lead us to certain experiences and places in life. The last several homes I lived in were guided directly by my intuition. One was in a small town in British Columbia, when, after the separation from my husband, I allowed myself a year sabbatical for healing. I decided in my mind I was not going to choose where I would live until a certain date in the future, as I wanted to give myself time to grieve. I opened myself up to being guided. One evening, riding on the back of my friend's motorcycle as we drove between a valley of mountains, I happened to notice a set of stairs leading up to a loft in a barn. Intuitively, a thought came from somewhere, telling me I could live there. Two weeks later, I mentioned to my friend that I could live in this little town, as the energy felt good to me. She mentioned how it was difficult to find a place to rent. Then she remembered her friend was moving and that her place above a barn might be available. I mentioned my intuitive insight. She asked me the color of the barn and I said it was grey. She stated that was her friend's place. She immediately made the phone call, and I was given the number of the property owner. I would also make a connection with a man who would play a significant part in transforming my life and teaching me what love was and what it was not.

A year later when I returned to live in northern Alberta, I received internal warning signs about a potential partnership I was moving towards. It only took a month and a half for me to see the bigger picture of how the partnership and I were not in alignment. I felt limited and no longer free in the space I was living, so I knew I needed my own place. I intuitively heard an inner message to call a guy I had recently met when I was searching for hay. His property had been for sale, and I wondered if it hadn't sold, he would be open to renting his house. At first, I called to ask to look at his place, thinking in the future I would be in the position to buy. He mentioned he was having an open house the following weekend. I did not make the open house that day and the next Wednesday I would hear very clearly at 8:00 a.m. to call this guy about his house. I picked up the phone, told him who I was, and asked if he would be willing to rent his house. His response was, which one? He then mentioned he had a barn-style home that his son had just moved out of. He and his wife were just talking about what they were going to do with it. I told him I was interested and asked if I could come to look. The barn-style home was 850 sq. ft. and the perfect space for me. It also had an amazing view of the prairies. I've always been grateful for the houses I've found by responding to my intuition. They were admired by me and my friends as perfect healing sanctuaries. I am open to seeing and hearing the signs of my inner guidance. I choose to listen. I learned my entire life has been guided. The more I trusted it, the more I felt safe, supported, and always protected. Everything always works out for me even when it is going against me.

How many times has your intuition guided you only to have you not listen and ignore your internal guidance? What does self-denial represent? A lack of trust or disbelief? Clearing limiting beliefs and aligning energy and money with values can help each of us refine how we use our energy while expanding our perception.

This alignment has attuned me to higher frequencies, signs, synchronicities and feelings of abundance. My experiences of energy and intuition have been elevated because I became more sensitive to energy, and I cultivated my sense of trust and belief in myself by praying to spirit.

Spirit communicates to us through intuition, books, symbols, and through the words of others. I will often feel a sensation of energy move over me and an inner knowing of what is right or wrong for me. I've had clients confess that they answered the call to reach out to me after seeing money conversations pop up everywhere, saying my words in videos were speaking directly to them. They felt a need to go deeper into their money relationships following their inner curiosity to understand more. The universe will offer up signs to say, "Hey, pay attention, I have something to reveal to you. I want you to take a closer look at this as there is something in this for you to learn or experience."

Archetypes are a guide to knowing ourselves. When we begin to know ourselves by understanding patterns and behaviors, as well as our emotions, we can change our course, breaking the chains rather than repeating the patterns of what we've done before. Hindsight can provide us with guidance. Are we willing to go deeper to do the work? The work is not for the faint of heart. You are more resilient than you might feel at this time. We can also relive the patterns differently using a higher perception, tuning in to live life more on our terms in alignment with God's path for us, which is to be a conduit for love. To access higher states of love we must move through our fear.

What does that look like for you? There are so many answers out in the world, and God knows sometimes we can be unclear in our feelings until we listen. If you are comprising what is right for yourself through some action (or inaction), you may be able to stay off course for a while; however, your inner voice will not stop until you hear its call.

Our emotions are our energy guides used to navigate from lower to higher energies, such as shame and guilt to joy or love. We can receive more of what we want, rather than what we do not want, but we must be clear and take action when we know for certain the path; otherwise we loop back. Each of us gets to become co-creators with spirit rather than trying to figure life out on our own. We can then arrive at a place where we feel more harmonious because we are in a place of alignment.

What we think about and the words we attach to those thoughts are powerful. Our emotions have power and are a source of energy. They can lead us to either take disempowered or empowered actions in the present moment, thus leading to the results that form our present lives. We need to ask: am I abusing my power? Or am I using my power for the good of myself and others? Yes, we know love hurts, and we hurt others, including ourselves. However, we can do better by being honest and not giving in to the compulsion to lie when we feel unsafe or not accepted.

If you are not happy with the results that are playing out in your life, pay attention to your emotions and ask, "What is it I need to let go of? What is it that I need to embrace more of?

There are many opportunities to experience abundance if we are open to receiving it. Abundance is within us. Some say it is our birthright because we are born into the world "enough." But then we live a life where many of the experiences shape a reality that makes us believe otherwise and we have to unlearn the damages pressed upon us. Our inner message too often is "I am not enough," and regrettably, we live in a world that supports the feeling of not having or being enough. We walk around too busy with life and are not grounded in who we are as spiritual human beings. The world can't make us conform when we know in our core that we are enough when we are connected inside to our truth. That comes because of deeper inner work and practices, such as yoga, meditation, journaling, or time spent in nature and prayer. Cultivating a daily practice has helped me immensely in staying plugged into my higher power and it leaves me grounded in *I am enough* each day. Prayer is a great way to anchor in protection and peace which I feel we need daily. It cultivates a strong foundation every day.

Beliefs that tell us we are not deserving enough, or worthy enough are simply not true. Who has given you this message? When frustrated, my mother stated, "You are just like your father." Did these words lead me to believe that there was something wrong with me? It was a predominant theme that showed up every time I wanted to leave my unhealthy relationship. Why would I want to leave my family, there must be something wrong with me. The truth is nothing was wrong with me, I was just unhappy inside myself and the relationship I was in at the time. My feelings were never validated, and I did not know that what I wanted mattered.

When we believe these lies about ourselves, we are separated from knowing our truth. The lies separate us from the connection to our higher power. The lies cast doubt, even shame, and we forget we are spiritual beings with the ability to connect the energy of higher frequencies which is found when we discover more of our truth.

We open to greater possibilities by expanding our perception and believing life will happen for us. We can open our minds and hearts to receive the lessons available for our growth by letting go of living the lie, shifting inwardly towards our truth, then choosing wisely to be in alignment with this truth, even if it means hurting another at the moment, because being honest sets you free. Otherwise, something else may hold authority over you which does not feel good. This awareness allows us the opportunity to live happier, healthier lives, free to be more of who we are.

Ask yourself, *What is the capacity of love if we live life to its fullest?* How does this feel for you? Women are such great givers, yet the biggest challenge for many of us is the receiving part. We need to let go of the patterns, the unexpressed emotions, and the lies. When we let them go, we create space in our bodies by expanding our capacity to be able to receive more. Being an over-giver or people-pleaser will provide clues to the imprints that we received as a child that are still playing out in our adult world because we have not yet received the lesson or released the negative emotion from the past, so it shows up as a challenge or opportunity in the present moment offering growth.

If you face the challenges and see them as an opportunity for you to know yourself, you will release and begin expanding your mindset, along with your capacity to create more. This is the key to accessing the abundance that is within you, the key that allows you to access more of the source energy through yourself.

My entire life I gave my heart and soul to men. I gave myself away easily, which left me feeling used or abused because inside I felt undeserving and not worthy of more. It never felt good, and it wasn't the type of love I was seeking. Going deeper allowed me to access the truth that *I am deserving and worthy of having my needs and wants met*. I am thrilled to live life now independent and free. I choose to give of myself with all of my heart and soul to live the will of God. I embody this truth more now than I have in the past. It requires practice. It was shown to me that while it can be received, it can also be lost by the choices I make each day, each moment.

The biggest shift occurs when I move from my thinking to what I want to feel in life. This process of moving from my head to my heart is the bridge. A profound shift occurred when I finally accepted and loved all parts of myself, including the dark places. This allowed me to access my *higher truth that I am worthy and deserving*. It shifted my internal compass, which also deepened my connection with God. I believe this is what my soul had been seeking all along. True connection. My soul would not let me stop searching until I deepened my connection to God and opened myself by clearing enough limiting beliefs and patterns so that my vessel or body could allow more of God's energy to be created through me. Many times, I have had to learn how to get out of my way. Many times, I felt like I was walking through quicksand because the energy of lies and limitations was too heavy.

Let go and let God, is a common saying. We do this by getting more grounded in who we are, feeling safe and secure inside, with a peaceful center despite what might be happening around us. We all have beliefs that have been imprinted upon us from family or society that are not in service to who we are or wish to become.

"Strive to become a millionaire, as it is not about the money; it is about who you will become along the way." This quote by Jim Rohn, one of my favorite philosophers, resonated with me when I first heard it. Clearing limiting beliefs can clear emotions that have been impressed upon us through past experiences. Our beliefs also impact our perception and how we view the world. Shedding a belief that doesn't serve us opens our perceptions, which in turn opens our hearts and minds. We begin to see opportunities in challenges with a more enlightened mindset.

As much as I feel I have an open mind, life always presents new opportunities to open it even more. Being open allows me to be in control of consciously choosing my choices versus reacting from an unconscious place within myself. I am more in control and live life more on my terms, which are keys to becoming prosperous. Letting go of the patterns that kept me trapped in the same cycles gave me free will and created space for the Divine's will to move through me. I will admit patterns or habits had to keep showing themselves until I was finally ready. I had to give myself the chance, over and over again, to let go with love and understanding rather than the all too familiar pattern of beating myself up. I recently noticed that it has been a long time since I felt like dying. Where did it go? This feeling used to visit me frequently over the years; however, the more I learned to love myself and live life in the present, with an open attitude about life happening for me, the more amazing experiences I could have. I no longer feel like wanting to end my life. It's because it no longer feels like hell.

Archetypes are symbolic metaphors, and they help us to understand the patterns and behaviors that show up in our lives. They have the power to shake us up and live life more empowered. Much like peeling away the layers of an onion, the unconscious part of ourselves will reveal more about us as we become grounded and secure with who we are. As we align to truths and connect to our authentic selves, we feel safe to experience life differently. It opens us up to take more responsibility and we grow by moving toward our souls' highest potential. Bringing the unconscious parts of ourselves into consciousness means living more in love and light versus in our fears. My healing journey focused on me and my life. Then I stepped into alignment with my heart and realized that my life was no longer about me. It opened me up to serve in bigger ways. I realized I would become an advocate for mental wellness because of my father and that my work would be a legacy for him, my family, and my role in offering guidance in the world. The work I do is about aligning right thinking, beliefs, and actions for the attainment of mental, emotional, physical, spiritual, and financial well-being and ending the internal struggles that can keep us trapped.

My husband used to say, "No one thinks like you." I would say, "Yes, I know people who think like me." The thing is, he did not think like me, and in the end, it would be our thinking, beliefs, and energy that would divide us. I would experience this in other relationships.

Think about that! Are your thoughts and beliefs creating a division within your life? What are the dominant feelings inside of you right now that are preventing you from being in a more loving state? Are you capable of delivering or receiving a message from a more mature place of love? Do you feel resentment, guilt, anger, or shame? Archetypes can deepen our self-awareness and change our unconscious behaviors so that we can become one with the source, ending the separation of our mind, body, and soul.

Do you ever wonder where your sense of striving comes from? Could it be from a place inside where you have something to prove, or you need to be approved of?

We serve and create from the unconscious parts of ourselves more than we realize and may continue to do so until we awaken fully or become one with our creator. Awakening is the process of clearing away lies that we have been holding as truths during our life journey. To find our truths, we must know ourselves and live our lives in alignment. We can begin the journey by seeing ourselves in relationship to others because everything is relational.

Even so, I sense that I need to walk alone for a while to strengthen who I am independent of another. I have also experienced that when shifts occur within me, they also occur outside of myself-in-relationship.

Habitual patterns are cracked open by doing deeper work and becoming more conscious of being who we are as we create more space for consciousness to evolve. By seeing our errors, we can atone for them through the right choices. Enlightenment means shining light into the dark parts of ourselves. It means we must love and accept those parts, too.

I can hold space for another person's parts by integrating my parts, the parts that make me whole. I cannot give to another what I haven't yet given to myself. I mentioned our thoughts lead to our feelings, which lead to action and our results to draw attention to the need for each of us to become accountable to and responsible for awakening our consciousness. Each of us can only move toward the co-creation of harmony by becoming aware of our potential as creators and using our energy appropriately for the greater good.

As I progress on my journey, my visions or intuitive insights allow me to stop being attached to anticipated outcomes and I am more open to receiving guidance along the way. I also have to pay attention to the messages I receive, as it may take some time for the guidance to work itself out. That is where prayer comes into play. If I can trust and hold space for what I asked for, then it will come to fruition.

Letting go of expectations or prescribed thoughts about how something will work out for us enables the universe to be more at play in our lives because we have released our resistance or the need to control. Things often turn out in ways we least expect, but if we are too attached to what we think must happen, we block ourselves from receiving and miss the opportunity that is directly in front of us. When we take the attitude of *this or something better,* it opens our pathways and allows us to go with the flow, receive guidance, and trust our inner knowingness.

Archetypes can be powerful insight tools to help us discover where we can grow and create a rich and meaningful life, to have our thoughts in alignment with higher more positive ways of thinking. This requires constant practice.

A Google search shows that people typically have an average of 50,000-70,000 thoughts a day. The question I asked myself was, "How many of my thoughts are negative?" Before I was aware of the impact of my negative thoughts, my life was a struggle. I was unhappy because my thoughts told me there was something wrong with me. I felt I was unlovable, and life mirrored this for me in an unhealthy relationship and harmful patterns or habits that, on more than one occasion, led me to want to end my own life thinking thoughts of suicide. I wanted things to change, but growing up, I did not have many positive role models. I had to work hard on myself to change what that first environment imprinted on me, which was a product of abandonment, lack of love, and unhealthy attention.

Our thoughts can fluctuate between negative and positive until we become more self-aware and reside in the moment. Then we can recognize the negative thought and shift it to a positive thought. This is the moment we begin taking back our power. There are several ways of changing our thought process. By being more present, journalling all emotions and thoughts, and researching leaders who inspire us so we can re-imprint ourselves with healthy ways of thinking and feeling. The wellness wheel of life helps show us the way. Ask yourself, "Who are you attracted to?" Many leaders have inspired me. Marianne Williamson is a long-time favorite as she teaches the universal principles of love anchored in Christian roots. Her messages have resonated with my soul for over two decades. I especially enjoy how she incorporates a metaphysical view of Bible meanings. It was metaphysics that opened my world to energy and healing.

Changing Your Story

We all have a money story, just like we have a life story. It is what we have been imprinted with by how we grew up, and what we experienced. For me to change this story, I had to discover the parts that imprinted what I no longer wanted to create. When I was a young girl, I recall a time when my father sent five dollars in an envelope. I was so excited, and while waiting to tell my mother I played rolling down a hillside with the money in my pocket. I lost the money and was devasted. I punished myself by saying I did not deserve to have the money. You can imagine the negative impact this story had on my relationship with money. Often, we have negative money memories, along with unexpressed emotions which create our wounds as adults.

Are there certain experiences that stand out for you? Can you see the role they might still be playing? These memories can rob you of opportunities for growth in new moments if you remain blind to the pattern.

To re-imprint ourselves is to take control of our thoughts and release the trapped emotional energy from the past. By applying new, positive practices, we create space to change our inner awareness and are adaptable so we can create shifts in the outer world. This results in changing our stories.

I'd been feeling an inner force awakening within me for some time. Then one day, while walking down the mountain road, my inner warrior showed up for the first time. She dropped into my body, and I could see before me the image of a beach. She arrived, ready to go to battle. Her hair was long, black, wavy, and flowing in the air. In her right hand was a long chain, at the end of the chain was a large mental ball covered with spikes. Before me, I saw the image of a man who played a role in awakening deep emotions. He represented fear and control. My inner warrior helped me know that I would fight for my life and my rights as a woman, rights I had previously and unconsciously given away. I called on my soul sisters, summoning their help, and knew this day would be the day to fight evil and take back our power. I grew tall. Towering over this man, I smashed him into the ground, declaring "You have no power over me." I continued to smash him fiercely, as I declared this over and over, clearing away his control and all his authority over me. The battle had been won or so I thought at that time. The real-life battle would soon present itself. This time I would be equipped with the strength of this warrior.

I instinctively knew it wasn't about this man. It was about the battle within myself, against my fears, my own manipulator and inner bully that had punished me far too long for things it had no right to. I thought for a moment that I may have crossed over a line and questioned my sanity. Released from the vision, I walked home, took a bath, and crawled into bed exhausted. Immediately after this battle in my inner world, a shift occurred in my outer world. Personal relationships ended and changed, and I knew it was a result of me winning the inner battle. I could no longer tolerate in relationships what I had tolerated for so long within myself. I started to put boundaries in place that were right for me. These were difficult for others to accept, and I severed ties with others who were too harsh with me. The experience was profound and is forever etched in my mind. This was the day I won the inner war.

Have you ever read a book and had the words feel like they were awakening an inner truth about yourself that you have yet to realize? I consider these moments as gifts from the spirit to guide you to a higher truth. The words resonate because they are accessing what you already know as the truth inside of you. You are recognizing some of your truth in reading my words. I want to encourage you to think and feel more for yourself, connecting more with what is right and true for your growth. Adolf Hitler once boasted, "What luck for rulers that men do not think." Imagine the harm you create for yourself and your life when you allow your faulty thinking to control your life by default. Too often, I have not listened to my truth, or my soul's calling, only to create more harm for myself and others. Truth is not easily accessed, but once you find it, you become more sensitive to what is untrue for you. Through a process of conscious awareness, you can live life by design, integrating the thoughts, beliefs, and actions that align with your soul's desires.

My desires for happiness were fulfilled as I grew in love, deepening my connection to God. I would learn what it takes to create and experience health in relationships by implementing boundaries, having open conversations, and feeling safe in doing so. I also experienced unhealthy relationships where I was not heard, understood, or felt safe which triggered deeper wounds. My triggers helped me take responsibility for my healing. I did not blame myself or another because that would have given away my power. Instead, I took back my power by seeing what my responsibility was and what the responsibility was of another.

I am not here to heal your stuff if you are not willing to see it.

Taking back my power gave me the freedom I was seeking. I had been seeking financial freedom in the pursuit of money; however, my desire would be achieved not by the balance of my bank account. Feeling free inside comes as a result of doing work that is in alignment with our internal truth and creating a story that aligns with that truth.

The negative imprints do not leave room for us to think and feel for ourselves or allow us to connect to abundance. They block the passageways to receiving and living a more prosperous life. They narrow our perceptions of life and our ability for a deeper connection. Our job is to clear the imprints so that we can evolve and be better humans, being and living more in the presence of love than in fear.

If you are seeking to change your story, I invite you to learn more about your unique archetypes and encourage you to take the free assessment which you can access on my website. www.janetkendrick.com. You will also find a self-study guide to begin your work.

Money as a Mirror

A client of mine expressed how she felt divided when giving money depending on the situation and the people involved. I asked her to talk about how she felt about giving. Her answer was a clear negative when it came to family members and the judgments surrounding past experiences brought to the surface the energy of resentment. When it came to her children, she felt giving was a gift that relinquished any attachments to receiving it back, so she gave freely. She considered giving to her children a gift and an honor that brought her great joy. Even when she would have conversations about being paid back the money, she had lent rather than given, she had to go into it with a clear mindset that it was a gift because of the family dynamics that played out when members of the family borrowed money. She felt that gifting allowed her to be free rather than feeling the constriction of "being owed" anything. My client was conscious about her relationship with money in this particular area however could see where she needed to clear some resentments from the past with family and also the value of where to put healthy boundaries in place with specific family members so that it felt more in alignment with her. Her way of giving freely was from an unconditional place. Even saying no, without any attached emotions gives the same unconditional feeling as it represents a healthy boundary for you. The feeling of people being indebted to you can make you feel like a martyr: "After all, look at all I have done for you." Being a martyr can lead you to a sense of superiority in a relationship which can cross the line for a power imbalance or lead to unhealthy expectations in your relationships with others. What have you done for me? Words expressed such as this can create a division in relationships because they are backed by control and manipulation rather than a place of love or understanding as well as from not having healthy boundaries in the present moment. When my grandmother passed, the small amount of money left behind was to be divided amounts the three sisters. Conflict arose when one sister took all the money creating an even bigger wedge in an already divided family, forging deeper wounds rather than healing. It wasn't about the money; the money was the mirror for the bigger problems that existed in the family relationships for years prior. The three sisters would continue to be divided and hate and resentment would grow. Long gone were the memories of love, joy, and laughter they had once shared. I am sure many of you reading this message have heard or felt the direct impact that money and death have created on people. It is not the money's fault. It's the wounds of the people involved that need healing and money can magnify the issues.

The type of giving expressed by my client is from an unconditional place of love and acceptance and comes from an open heart. This opens us to receive more love and is important for the health and happiness of us as individuals and in relationships. It is when we give from this heart space that we open more to feelings of joy by reciprocity we receive what we give into the world. This can allow our inner nurturer to feel stronger, more alive, and energized. The relationship between the sisters was layered with conditions and hurts of the past which blocked love, and joy, and in such a vulnerable time where the death of my grandmother could have provided an opportunity for healing. My grandmother would not experience or witness the healing within her own children. When my mother was diagnosed with terminal cancer, she expressed her desire for my brothers and me to communicate and come together before she died. When you are given five years left to live, you begin to look at all your relationships differently, including your relationship with money. Your heart tends to soften and people you once discarded may be looked at with more value. The problem with money is that sometimes you tend to value it more than the people in your life. Money alone has the power to create great distance between loved ones, and it is worth asking, is it the money or the beliefs, attitudes, and behaviors of people that need changing? The solution is to have the tools and courage needed for tough conversations in those difficult moments when hurts occur. Such conversations could to stop the hurt and establish healthy habits and patterns.

Another unhealthy money pattern occurs when women find it difficult to set financial boundaries with people they care about. Too often women say yes when they really want to say no or allow themselves to be taken advantage of financially by others, secretly feeling resentful because what they give is not reciprocated. Money can be a powerful mirror for women showing them the ways they give away their power or remain disempowered rather than being able to feel empowered. How do you feel about your money relationship? Right now, is there a habit or pattern you would like to let go of? Acknowledge whatever surfaces. Take a moment to offer a prayer to ask for guidance in letting go or journal for a deeper reflection of the image that money is mirroring for you.

When women begin to take care of their own money, they are also taking care of themselves and their financial foundation. We take time to pull out the weeds that clog our foundation and then seal the cracks. And if we take on too much, that may be because being busy is a form of denial or avoidance.

You are your greatest asset and when you see the value in who you are and recognize the sacredness of energy within, it will also be mirrored in healthy relationships, including money. Begin to use money as a tool that is expressed in ways that are important to you and your values and you will feel freer as your fruits change because you have stopped giving away your energy to what is robbing you of your worth and value.

When a friend of mine told her husband he would have to make his share of the household rent in the upcoming month, or she would have to find a new roommate, it set her free from growing resentment and anxiety. She had previously avoided speaking up for what was important for her in a relationship. Her needs were not being met when she over-supported her husband and sacrificed herself because she lacked a clear boundary. She kept denying herself by not acknowledging her truth and what her negative emotions were trying to reveal to her. She was tolerating his childish ways, and it was robbing her and him of joy and happiness. She was finally able to say that while she accepted that he is on his path, she chooses to no longer over-support him in this way with money; however she will support him in other ways. It created space for positive growth in their relationship. When he heard her, for the first time, it was hard. The pain of shame set in. I encouraged him to feel it, to allow it to motivate him to act and change his patterns and the behaviors that were holding him back. A week later, he processed his experience by forgiving himself and immediately attracted an opportunity for the rent he now wanted to be responsible for. He stopped tolerating his own childish behavior and she, hers. Their relationship grew again, and they began to act more as a team. In this process, he also uncovered a deeper belief that he would have to sacrifice his family if he achieved wealth. He acknowledged how much he acted like a little bitch when things did not go his way. Although he was a visionary trying to grow a business, he needed to clear this imprinted belief and behavior, as it did not serve the man he wanted to become.

As women feel empowered to do better in the world, they must begin by recognizing their unique gifts and strengths. Having healthy boundaries helps women know when to say yes or no . We are always making choices for ourselves and when we take a moment to connect inwardly and process where we are giving from, we can make an empowered choice whether it is a yes or no without negative energy emotions being attached to it. Taking responsibility and making a choice is extremely empowering even if it feels difficult or uncomfortable in the moment. There is a balance between giving to someone and not robbing them of their power. It is important to avoid taking responsibility for something not in your control. Saying no to them and allowing another opportunity to take responsibility is empowering for both individuals. Otherwise, being an enabler just allows behaviors to repeat that might be holding the other person back. Creating codependency in relationships is not healthy. Denying yourself what is right for you is not healthy for you, it only creates more of what you don't want.

Opportunities come to us every day. Because every day is a new experience, and because we cannot control the actions of other people, we are left to control our actions. By knowing our patterns we can create positive or negative results in the present. What we do today will create our tomorrows. Opportunities are filtered through the lens of our archetypes, our stories, patterns, beliefs, and past experiences.

In one moment, we can make a choice or decision that can activate a powerful shift that will create a ripple effect across all areas of our lives. Knowing our archetypal patterns allows us to empower our strengths and consciously manage our challenges so that we are no longer running our lives unconsciously. When we are not trying to be someone we are not and are not acting from the shadow side of ourselves, we take off the mask. We can be our authentic selves, which is an act of self-love because it aligns us with our truth. By letting go of the lies and being honest, we are real, and healing comes as we become whole.

In the previous paragraphs, I have shared moments where the shadow or ego side of self shows up in our money relationships. Many of us spend our moments chasing a moving money target, and as it happens when we chase something, it runs away from us. We are always in pursuit without ever retrieving it. Or when we do achieve it without healing inside, we still feel it's not enough. This means we will never be satisfied with the amount of money we have. When we feel there is never enough money, it indicates hidden fears that are robbing us of feeling free.

What is the belief that is inside of you that says repeatedly that there is not enough? Are you willing to explore this belief to let it go? The shadow parts of ourselves show up when we feel the need to rescue others, abandon ourselves, feel resentful, or become martyrs. This can be reflected in our money relationship when we feel a lack of financial independence, and no matter how much money we have, we remain disempowered and lack the inner sense of true freedom. We do not come from lack and lack would be the lie that separates us from our truth.

How often do you feel overwhelmed with the basics of financial details? How much energy is drained with flamboyant spending, avoiding anything to do with finances, or spending to mask feeling undeserving, unappreciated, or unloved? Another aspect of being in the shadow side is when you keep secrets, or deceptions behind your actions. Do you gamble with financial security, or get caught in the need to win the approval of others? Remember, you are always creating, and the question to ask is "What source am I creating from?"

I make sure to check in and ask myself this question when I make a decision regarding my life or career. I want to be sure I am creating from a place of love, connecting to the will of God and my sacred strengths. Too many times my mind can trick or confuse me, and when it tries to create doubt or retreat from what it is I want to create, it never feels good. I realign my thoughts in my prayers to God to create the pathway I desire, releasing through tears and moving forward. Negative thinking, beliefs or wrong actions are not in alignment with my truth or what I want to create or rather what God's will want to co-create through me.

The love side of self, the empowered, inspired, or light side of self is the place where we can make choices that will shift us away from or move through the shadow side—the fear side, the insecure part of self, the incessant doubting side. We become whole by accepting all parts of self, both positive and negative like a dance between the energies. When we judge or condemn what we feel as negative or the dark side of self, we punish ourselves. It is liberating when we end this duality by accepting it. Rather than beat ourselves up over what we perceive as mistakes, instead, we can see experiences as opportunities. Learning this allows us to grow and empowers new choices from a higher place within. It also creates a huge shift in our consciousness as we witness that moment when we are in a fear state. This allows us to give ourselves the attention we need and move through it. Our awareness of ourselves as both light and dark, positive, and negative, able to both love and hate is the only way to see what we need to see. Looking back at past experiences as an adult with an open mind and unbiased perception allows us to retrieve the lesson we may have missed because the pattern is still repeating itself. The negative imprints we receive as children can impact us as adults if they haven't been expressed or understood. To bring light to a situation is to bring understanding. As adults, we are still imprinting ourselves and it takes a very strong sense of awareness of ourselves. Once we recognize who we are and what our gifts and energy mean, we begin to see how we have to hold it as sacred. To be our whole self is to be all of ourselves with acceptance and love. It is not always easy to achieve because our minds and beliefs need to be uprooted to create change so we can live more in a state of love than fear.

When I read the verse in the Bible that Jesus paid the price for our sins and made us free, it hit me. Being a child of God, I looked to him and never really took the time to understand Jesus as a holy spirit who came back to set us free. What I now understand is that freedom is found when we are open to receiving the holy spirit or a higher power. We connect to our enlightened net worth by letting go of our sins or our liabilities. We also sin when we *miss the mark*, are *out of alignment*, and are *not in integrity with our truth, our higher selves*. This blocks the channel for spirits to have access and create through us. When we are in integrity, we tell the truth, are free of judgment, shame, and guilt, we are open to more love, joy, prosperity and abundance. It is God's grace that is within us that we can transcend above these lower energies that rob us of what we seek. This is our birthright as God who is love, created us in love and loved us so much that he allowed his son, Jesus Christ to die for us, only to return in spirit to which we can access. We need to let go of what blocks us from receiving it. Right now, take a moment to ask yourself, what is blocking you from receiving? Ask for guidance in releasing whatever it is. If you are willing to take action on the answer you receive, you will find peace and freedom from what holds you back. Breathe deeply, give thanks and breathe out. Let go.

We are born enough. Experience imprints us and separates us from our truth.

I always bought into the story that there was something wrong with me. As adults, when we are facing challenges, we often react from a place of emotions that have yet to be released or healed. Many times, it is our inner child that needs to be acknowledged or consoled. This is when you sit your inner child on your lap and have a conversation to give her some understanding of the experiences that made her believe she was unworthy or somehow deserved to be punished back then. What is your inner child trying to tell you? Ask her, or him and listen to what comes up for you. From a compassionate and loving place, what would you say to them? Through awareness and understanding, we can find forgiveness for those around us and more importantly, for ourselves in the moment. Just as God has forgiven us for our sins, so must we forgive ourselves. Forgiveness opens us to love, and we begin to feel more compassion and kindness toward our adult selves. With this new information, we can now empower new choices. This is deeply healing and allows us to make decisions that will move us forward as leaders in our lives, relationships and business or careers.

Are you currently held hostage or divided within by an unconscious pattern from an experience or unexpressed emotions? Are you too far in your past or too far in the future to be connected to this present moment, causing you to miss opportunities of abundance that might be right in front of you? At this moment, from a place of connection, say out loud: "I trust. I am asking. I am receiving, I am speaking from this place of truth in alignment with my higher self now. I can make a choice that is an empowered yes. Or an empowered no." If fear shows up, lean into it for growth and to honor yourself. To honor your soul. What is fear trying to show you? Practice being more present, give attention and care to practices that ground you in the morning to establish your foundation for the day. Pause before eating, smell your food. Give your body choices, and affirm what you need today. Give it to yourself. You are valuable and worthy of living your best life as your best self. Pause here, to acknowledge this truth. If you do not feel it, be gentle and acknowledge your purpose is to discover more of who you are. The key to your happiness is to live your truth.

Life in Fragments

We all need to ask how often we trade temporary discomfort for long-term dis-ease?

There have been many times throughout my life when I failed to express what I wanted and said yes when I wanted to say no, leaving me in a place of indecision. I did not know my value. I had to learn this valuable lesson each time I chose to go against the desire of my soul. It created a profound negative impact on my life and the loved ones around me. Not listening also became a catalyst to listening because I felt the impact on a subconscious level which revealed itself as I did deeper healing work to understand why I was having a certain experience. Hindsight provided clues. By looking back at what had occurred, and how, I can see that if I had only listened to myself, I could have prevented such pain.

My first marriage ended around April 2009 and several months later I met the man that would become my second husband. I had left my first marriage with no alimony, and no financial support because

I just wanted peace. I wanted out of the unhealthy marriage and finally found the courage to get off that path. I left with half the debt. Because I had been a stay-at-home mom for many of those years, I found myself completely starting over. It took a lot of courage for me to leave, and I was not ready to make a lot of empowered decisions on my own during that time. Things happened that shook my world and survival was the main focus for several years to follow. My new boyfriend had a strong desire to protect me, and he suggested that I move in with him. It made sense financially, even though we had only known one another for six months. I said yes, even though I'd mentioned at the beginning of our dating that I wanted to be on my own for at least a year before getting into a committed relationship. My children were living with their dad, and I didn't see them for three years. After a year of living with my boyfriend, I was a deeply hurt and wounded mother. On a soul level, I wanted to get my place to make it easy for the girls to come to see me. I approached the subject of getting a place of my own while we were out for an evening horseback ride. I simply said, "I feel like I should get my place. I want the girls to have easy access to being with me and I do not want to live here."

His immediate response was, "You are either in this or not." I did not want to leave our relationship; I just wanted my own place. I stayed, against my own soul's desire, because I thought leaving would create more harm. The energy in the house changed. Each time on my drive home from work, I would think, *I do not want to go home*. I would put my hand on the doorknob to enter and I would think, *I do not want to be here*. My relationship with my stepsons declined as I did not want to be in their company. The energy in the room would feel heavy and restricting and I couldn't understand it at the time. I wanted to be with my children. I also did not know at that time the extent of the trauma and abuse my children were being subjected to.

Fast forward years later, I was seeking answers to why I felt the way I did when I realized how I imprinted myself with these negative thoughts and emotions and later discovered a reason why I never became a financial contributor to the house: *I never wanted to be there.* I did not listen to my own emotions and the warning signs my energy provided for me. I later realized how disempowered I was in my rights as a mother and a woman because I avoided standing up for myself. At the same time, I was too often a victim of men who held authority over me. I had yet to see my value and they mirrored it.

This was one moment of our relationship where I did not honor myself and the impact was detrimental. It could have been prevented. What would have been different if we'd had an open conversation about needs and feelings? We might have stayed together. I do consider the twelve years we shared as one of my healthiest relationships. His archetype was a strong protector and I always felt safe. Our relationship provided the foundation that would allow me to grow internally in security and safety. The relationship was stable and unthreatening, which was important for reshaping my inner foundation.

Growth requires a safe space. Without psychological or emotional safety in life, it's challenging to survive, let alone thrive. When I began my career in life insurance and I struggled to believe in myself, it was my husband who said, "Janet if you do not believe in yourself, who will believe in you?" Of course, his question took me inward to explore the reason why I did not believe in myself. I would spend six days walking in nature, meditating and journalling to get to the root cause of why I did not believe in myself. The deep-rooted belief revealed itself: *I was not enough.* I was born in an environment where I was placed for adoption twice before 6 months of age. This environment did not enable the expression of love and it imprinted me with a deep sense that I was not enough. I was ready to let this lie go as I knew the truth. I was born enough. I was created by my Father, God who is love, born of love. Once I recognized the root cause I followed it up with a hypnotherapy session. My root chakra healed, and I knew I was enough. Two years later, my husband would announce I was no longer the woman he married, and he did not like the woman I had become. He felt I was on my path, but he was no longer going to be a part of it. I needed to leave. Leaving a healthy relationship would prove to be easier than leaving an unhealthy one. Don't get me wrong, we had challenges and there would be pain. However, it was respectful, and I allowed space for grieving as we parted ways.

Life would show me more. Years later, I encountered the same feeling of not wanting to be in a place. This time I recognized the unexpressed emotions and rather than staying where my soul felt limited, I left. I spent only months in a place rather than years as I answered the calling of my soul without hesitation. I left the mountains of British Columbia and returned to northern Alberta with an opportunity to make one of my dreams come true. The offer was to potentially begin a women's wellness healing center with horses. The facility was high class and I got to live in a grand space. I felt extremely blessed and it mirrored the abundance that I had tapped into.

My work at the center involved working with someone very different from me. From the beginning, expectations were not clear, but I was willing to go with it. Finally, after having many conversations with this person, I realized that I did not feel valued. I walked away from a conversation where I was being disrespected with rude words. When I woke up feeling limited and trapped, I honored my soul's calling and immediately found a new place for myself. Instead of repeating a pattern of not listening to my soul, I acted and moved in a new direction. I moved toward freedom. Hindsight also showed me that had I expressed how I felt, and if I'd had deeper conversations, I could have prevented what happened that led me into a life of fear for some time; however, life is a journey and the lessons we can learn about ourselves can be illusive and deeply buried. And yet, as long as we feel safe in bringing the unconscious parts of ourselves to light and becoming more conscious, ultimately we become better human beings.

Expanding our self-awareness can be both exciting and scary at the same time. We easily repeat our unconscious patterns until we are truly ready to stop the cycle and consciously make new choices to live in alignment with what we truly desire. We have to get serious about who we are. It takes knowing our value and worth and a willingness to stop tolerating the behaviors that got us in the position in which we no longer wish to remain.

The power of understanding our archetypes is to stop living life unconsciously. We become more conscious, recognizing the sacredness of this power, and take it back by making integral choices and walking the right path. I compare it to the image of an iceberg. The ten percent above the water is our thinking mind, while the ninety percent below the surface is considered our subconscious or unconscious mind– the captain of our ship. This is where our beliefs, attitudes, and imprints come into play. We can explore more truth about ourselves when we are ready to move to the next levels within; until then our subconscious or ego-self is going to protect us because it wants to keep us safe. We can retreat to old habits, darkness or move forward creating a new life in the direction of light and love as ourselves, right now, anchored in the truth, I am *enough*.

Marianne Williamson writes "It is our light, not our darkness that frightens us the most." It is when we face the darkness, the fears, and the beliefs, that we are enlightened and rise to higher parts of ourselves. When we tend to be judgmental towards others, our emotional triggers can provide clues to where deeper work is required. Our triggers are mirrors of the qualities within ourselves that need acknowledgment and acceptance. What we are annoyed by in another person is often a quality we deny within ourselves. When we judge, we can avoid looking at ourselves. We need to ask, *What is it that bothers me about this person?* Why do we feel the need to judge? Judging is an indication that we are projecting our discomfort upon someone else. By looking inward to observe the parts of ourselves that are judging we can see ourselves on another level. What insecurities or fears are we projecting? We do not need to know what is going on inside someone else. Our job is to look closer at what is going on inside ourselves when we are triggered by another. If we can accept that judgments give away our energy, we can stop projecting. This will provide an opportunity to use our words and thoughts to create more kindness and compassion within ourselves, and we will extend this energy toward others. When we acknowledge the qualities that may be irritating us by seeing how they are reflected in us, as well, we become more aligned with our soul and the qualities of kindness and compassion that we are here to illuminate. It also fosters oneness, because we can integrate the qualities within ourselves that need acknowledgment which is the reason for us being triggered by the qualities of another. For a deeper understanding of how others can mirror the parts of ourselves that we reject or don't acknowledge, also known as our shadow sides, I recommend that you read Debbie Fords' book The Dark Side of the Light Chasers. When you recognize yourself in others you can be more aware of when someone is projecting on you.

When we are ready or feel a sense of inner safety, more will be revealed so that we can grow towards the next levels of ourselves by understanding and accepting who we are on a whole level. The release of energy comes through tears, and a wide range of emotions, such as laughter, whatever is not in service to us, our body, and the soul parts of us that love truth and seek to live it in reality. Our body also provides clues. Whenever I feel constipated, I know there are old beliefs, patterns, or ideas that I need to let go of. If I get heartburn, it lets me know I am in fear. When I am in a place of indecision, my gums swell. I practice being gentle as I listen to what my body is telling me and take the steps to honor myself by giving myself the love, space, and attention that my body, mind, and soul require to grow. I practice yoga and affirmations to let go of my past so that I can embrace my life fully now. When my body lets go as I honor myself. I feel happier and freer as I let go and flow.

When something speaks to you on an emotional level or physical level, allow your energy to move, breathe deeply, and allow the process to unfold. Trust your inner wisdom. Remember, healthy people feel. Honor what you think and feel by saying "I value myself, and what I have to say matters." When you choose to ignore your inner calling, what is the message you are expressing to yourself? If you are not listening to yourself, what you are communicating is that what you have to say has little or no value. How often do you find yourself devaluing who you are or what you feel?

Be gentle here! It can be difficult to face emotions and it is not something we are taught. I teach in classrooms where teens tell me they are not good at talking about their feelings. It is a common thread, for me, growing up in a household that did not know how to express love easily also meant they lacked the proper tools to discuss other emotions. Addictions, such as alcohol or drugs, offer a temporary escape from uncomfortable feelings by numbing ourselves. An addiction such as drugs or alcohol, gambling, debt, or an imbalance of power in a relationship can have authority over you which becomes a liability for a whole sense of self. It robs you of your ability to be in higher states of love. What you lack within yourself is what you will attract in relationships. Everything in life is relational, and when you consciously decide to work through challenges in life by focusing on your strengths and moving through heavier emotions, you create enormous synchronicities. By creating a change in your emotional, energetic state, you are saying to your higher power, I trust you and I know I am supported. When you release and open the pathways, you can see synchronicities. Your energy shows up differently in the world as a result of showing up for yourself from a different place.

Your ability to experience energy may also change. The more I grew in love, the more negative energies could not be tolerated, and it became necessary to put up a healthy boundary. In the past, lacking boundaries was too familiar because I had not yet discovered my value or felt a deeper sense of self-worth. Healthy boundaries are an expression of love as you see yourself as sacred where protection and self-respect are required. The more you awaken by knowing yourself, the more you will see with an open, expanded perception of yourself, others, and the world. You will not be the same; you will be the better version of yourself. Are you ready for that? Take a moment right now to observe what the better you looks like. What do you look like? Are you radiant as you embody your humble magnificence? How do you feel in this moment? Are your shoulders back, the heart opened, and head high with a gentle confidence? What are you doing and who are you spending time with? Give your best self some attention. You are worthy. Take a breath; repeat, *I am worthy of living my best life.*

On the other hand, if you are not fully awakened to higher emotions about yourself, you might feel a sense of separation, disconnected, lost, confused, or depressed, you might be asking yourself, *What is wrong with me? There must be something wrong with me. Why am I not satisfied or why do I want more?* Additionally, you might find yourself lamenting over not being happy with what is, and you may compare yourself to others, which opens the door for more self-criticism or judgments. This can be the beginning of your search and is okay to want more. I am grateful for wanting more than what the beginning of my life provided me. I am grateful that I learned I was perfectly normal. It was the stirring of my spirit calling me home. I resonated with Louise Hays's description of depression as a symptom of not listening to one's soul. Lousie's book Heal Your Body teaches you how to listen to your body and the symbols it creates to provide insights into how it communicates to us on a deeper level. The soul in you wants to awaken to self, to grow up and feel more love and joy, rather than negative emotions that rob you of your precious life force. Your soul triggers within you the desire for more. I used to be chastised for never being satisfied but it was the soul in me that was hungry and seeking answers to understand my life and how to make it better.

In her book, Lousie wrote about depression as a message of not listening to your soul. I resonated with her meaning and depression lost its power over me as I changed my thoughts and took steps to heal my life. I believe the *more* we seek is the connection to this internal love, allowing us to know ourselves so that we can embody this truth. Everything else is a lie.

Love is found when you connect with your Source - GOD. Connecting your mind body and spirit in alignment with living your truth is to live more in the state of love, with an inner sense of freedom to express your unique gifts and talents free from the fears, ideas, and limitations that want to hold you back from more growth.

Working in my business as a Prosperous Woman Coach has allowed me to inspire others to heal and take their power by understanding themselves and the role their emotions play. I felt in alignment. I stopped searching, having found exactly what I was looking for in this type of work and it fueled my sense of purpose. It provided me with what I had been seeking in a career. I will keep changing jobs that are not in alignment with my soul's purpose to heal and inspire others to do the same.

You will know when you are ready for more because you'll hear this inner calling that will not stop. You will see physical signs that let you know. The question is will you listen to your inner voice of intuition that is asking you to change? The leap of courage comes with ease and grace as you move forward empowered with strength, your energy-infused spirit free to move toward more growth. Keep going, this is the time for growth and forward movement. Trust that you are moving to the next levels within yourself and toward higher levels of consciousness. You got this!

The Energy of Our Bodies

**When we are deep in the trenches of feeling shame or blame,
we are in an unbalanced state.**

Energy work helps address the balance and flow of energy through the body. There are many kinds of energy work. Yoga practice unites the mind, the body, and the soul. Chakras are the energy centers in our body that can be balanced or unbalanced. Not feeling your emotions blocks your chakras which can cause your body to store emotions. Yoga postures move the body and its energy, releasing stuck emotions and stress in the body so we can come more into alignment with our higher self because we allow ourselves the opportunity to get quiet and to practice listening to what our inner self is trying to express. By connecting to breath, we connect with our life force which allows us to feel more grounded in the present. Begin breathing more consciously by feeling how deeply your breath enters your body, whether it is in your chest or lower belly, to find your center and get grounded in who you are.

Take a moment right now to place your hand on your chest and notice how deep or shallow you breathe into your body. Do this with no judgment to learn the pattern of your breath. Are you breathing fully and deeply into the parts of your life that matter?

I have enjoyed the different breathing practices that allow me to move into deeper places within myself and feel myself expanding with my energy body. Energy work, such as breathe work or reiki, can also assist in letting go of the lies that separate us from our truths. Being more present in the moment allows a connection with our spiritual energy, forming a deeper peace and greater love while creating a union between the mind, body, and soul. This leads us to feel more whole and aids the process of healing. Healing allows us to recognize the differences in how we feel, such as the changes I experienced when I shifted my life from feelings of depression and despair to happiness, and healthier relationships leading to an increased sense of freedom. Healing work created space internally for more freedom as I let go of negative thinking, releasing feelings of shame and the need to punish myself. Doing the inner work created different results in my outer world as I became a better guide to myself because I became more informed about the emotional energy in my body and what it was communicating to me. I was able to create a better life by letting go of an old story that no longer served my higher self; energy work helped me along the way.

CHAKRAS

The root chakra is located at the base of the tailbone, and it represents our connection to our family, our tribe. It also connects us with money and abundance, our right to be here, to be enough, to feel safe, to feel secure. When we grow up in an environment that is not safe or secure, or if we have past experiences that harmed us, our healthy development of self can be interrupted. Now we must heal those wounded parts of ourselves and get grounded in who we are, growing and trusting that it is safe to be authentic. Again, we need to be grounded and supported, to know we have the right to be here and that we are enough as we are, to feel safe and secure, independent of anything that is happening externally. I invite you to explore Adverse Childhood Experiences (ACES)[2] which are the potentially traumatic events that can occur in childhood, such as violence, abuse, and growing up in a family with mental health or substance use problems. Toxic stress experienced as a result of ACES can change brain development and affect how the body responds to stress. I received this information in a crisis training around intimate-partner violence. It was extremely eye-opening and gave me a greater understanding of my life and why healing was imperative for my growth. Refer to the endnotes for more information and to take the assessment to discover your score. It may provide insights into your life as an adult and areas where you struggle. Getting grounded in who you are is important.

---

2 https://www.acesaware.org/wp-content/uploads/2022/07/ACE-Questionnaire-for-Adults-Identified-English-rev.7.26.22.pdf

I have covered a lot about connection with a higher power. Here, I will reference how Alcoholics Anonymous (AA) was founded on connection to a power greater than self. My grandfather was a member, and when I was a young girl he would take me to Al-Anon meetings. I was an empathic child, and these meetings triggered many emotions. Often, I would sob uncontrollably for hours. I read (and invite you to explore) *The Map of Consciousness* by David R Hawkins, MD, Ph.D. His scientific studies measured the frequency of low energy vibration of alcoholics in the early stages of recovery and how it shifts as they work the twelve steps, which is a healing modality. AA recommends addicts simply show up, and the energy of others engaged in the work will eventually have a positive impact on them, lifting them higher until they can do it themselves. Many individuals express feeling resistance because they don't believe in God, but as the addictive individual opens to a new perspective within themselves, they open up the pathways to receive a higher power and higher energy frequencies that are life-transforming.

In the book *Heal your Life* by Louise Hay, she writes that *addiction is running away from self*. What are you running away from? The truth of who you really are is not what you have conformed to be in this world. When you stop running and look at your experiences from a more expanded view, your lens changes. Now you see your experiences as a gift as you heal to become the better version of yourself. Pause for a moment to acknowledge, *It is safe to be me*. This place of safety is attainable by making different choices. Be gentle with yourself as you build a more solid foundation and repair the damage that may have been created in your early childhood.

Our sacral chakra is associated with our feelings, pleasure, sexuality, and our ability to tap into creativity when procreating in life, whether it is art or business. Feelings also tie us to family, sometimes in ways that are not in alignment with our highest good. The element here is water: our emotions that ebb and flow freely or not. In what ways can you learn to go with the flow in life's experiences? We can do this by "witnessing" our emotions, and asking ourselves, *What am I feeling in this current situation. Love or fear? Am I secure, or am I feeling disempowered?* Such questioning doesn't mean avoiding, running away or retreating to a place of self-punishment. I like to say *when in doubt, lay about*, meaning wait to respond. Pause to collect your thoughts before you speak. Permit yourselves to say, "I need more time to think about it before I respond." When looking at your money relationship, what are you feeling, what is it that you want to happen in your money relationship? Guilt can often be an enemy here. However, healthy guilt signals to the body that you are going against yourself or something you value.

I recall feeling guilt in my body the evening I went on the Tinder app and engaged in a conversation with someone I thought could have been the guy I had been seeing because of the similarities. I felt guilt in my sacral chakra, and a sensation in my heart that told me, "I am not over this guy." Mentally and emotionally, he was still in my being. I immediately deleted the app and decided not to go down that rabbit hole. I was not ready for a relationship. Another time I felt a healthy sense of guilt when a friend loaned me money as I was short of funds. I paid the bills I needed to, then used some of the money to sign up for a seven-week yoga class. During the class, I felt the same sensation in my heart and sacral, and when I looked closer, I realized that I went against what I valued, which was my relationship. I immediately knew that my action would create harm because I *unconsciously, impulsively* chose to sign up for this class. I saw the bigger picture and how often I repeated this action in my life, impulsively reacting rather than consciously making choices in my relationships, life, or around money regarding what I valued more. Our money is an extension of how we use our energy and when done in alignment with our values and beliefs we create the synchronicities that we want to in life rather than what we don't want. This time I was able to address my guilt by asking for a refund and dropping the class. I already had a solid practice of my own and I didn't need to spend more money by taking a class.

Ask yourself, how many ways do you spend your money that are not in alignment with what you really want in life? How do you feel about your spending patterns or about money in general? Your feelings will provide you with deeper insights. If you say you want something badly but take action in the opposite direction, it is unlikely that you are feeling in harmony or in sync with your relationship. Perhaps you can see the pattern repeating but feel powerless to change it, and instead you feel frustrated or depressed because you are moving further away from what you really want in life. This is the moment where you look up and ask for help. Open yourself to receive by releasing the hurts and habits that keep you stuck in a cycle of unhappiness, unhealthy relationships with yourself, or money. Breathe in and say: *I forgive myself for my past mistakes. I am willing to begin again.* This is why money is such a powerful teacher. Check-in often and ask this question: Am I using money in alignment with what I value and want to create in life? Is it possible that you do not see the value of yourself, or feel you are worthy of achieving more?

Think of a time when you committed to not spending or to pay off your debt only to keep going against yourself. Apply forgiveness and anchor in the belief that *I can choose my life, I am capable, creative, and powerful to complete my goals.* Create a space for prayer where you ask for help daily. In Philippians 4:6-7 it says: "Do not be anxious about anything, but in every situation, by prayer and petition, with thanksgiving, present your request to God. And the peace of God, which transcends all your understanding, will guard your hearts and minds in Christ Jesus". Whatever you feel is your higher power, pray to it daily.

The power of prayer has been a constant throughout my life, and the more I changed from living from fear to love, the more my life transcended and I achieved more of what I was seeking. I live my life in an abundance of love, peace, and calm. The feelings of having to continually strive harder and always having something to prove have been changed to having more patience and peace. I live in the presence of now, and this reward to me is extreme abundance.

Guilt is an enemy for women if it's an instant reaction to anything and everything we do. Women feel guilty as mothers being in business for themselves, or we feel guilty about not doing enough or doing too much. Guilt robs us of feeling joyful, deserving, or worthy, which can affect our income and the level of happiness we experience in life. We can reframe this guilt when it shows up by saying, "Of course, this is happening *for* me. I am deserving. I am worthy. I am creating my life using my intuition and releasing the guilt that no longer serves me." A healthy amount of guilt can let us know when we are going against ourselves. Knowing this difference is empowering. Notice where you might be lacking in your feelings. This could represent root chakra issues. A strong foundation is essential.

Moving up into our solar plexus, we find our self-esteem, our connection to an inner sense of being on purpose in our lives. This is our fire in the belly, connecting us to the source of our empowerment or passion about the things that motivate us to get out of bed in the morning. Take a moment to go a little deeper. Ask yourself: *Am I living the divine's will or somebody else's will? Am I listening and trusting my inner guidance? Does someone or something have authority over me that is preventing me from feeling completely free in my life and achieving what matters to me? Are there unconscious beliefs that no longer serve my highest good that make me react before I am clear about what is right for myself? Do I believe that I am not good enough because of what someone else wants or expects from me, or because I have made choices in the past about money, debts, and current beliefs that tell me I am not good enough, and it has authority or power over me?*

All of these questions pose a liability that robs you of your enlightened net worth and the answers can help you take back your power. A lot is going on in our solar plexus, which is also connected to the subconscious. The good news is when you are feeling a healthier sense of self-esteem, you also feel more inclined to take empowered action. When you lead your life more courageously, you become more confident.

In a high state of love, I can move through the challenges that life brings with grace and ease. This means I am doing things politely and making difficult things less difficult because I am accessing my power and using it for good.

When you are aware of the moment your shadow parts show up, you can choose to consciously move through them by taking the right actions in honor of the life you want to create. You must acknowledge the parts of yourselves that want to hold you back. You can see them, and then you can choose not to punish yourself by accepting them for what they are, without judging them as good or bad. Instead, you can acknowledge that you are going to support and nurture yourself through whatever you are presently experiencing. By igniting more courage, and more confidence, you can step forward even more as a leader rising from a powerful, positive space. You play smaller when you doubt yourself or fail to trust your inner wisdom because you are afraid of that growth, afraid of stepping into your highest potential.

There is a place that is waiting for you to arrive. When you know you are ready for more, the subconscious will reveal more of what you need to let go of so that you can be free from that which holds you back. It's okay to be afraid because our fears are a natural part of who we are, and our ego wants to protect us and keep us safe. I consider this as the duality that separates us and prevents us from being one with God or spirit. This is where doing clearing work in the lower chakras is important to become more grounded in who we are without being influenced by others or our fears. We can be truer to ourselves by being our power.

In yoga, which is about living in alignment, when we are out of balance, we must go within to do the deeper work of chakra clearing. We can find understanding by looking at past experiences that may be impacting us negatively in the present and seeing the lesson or opportunity and offering up forgiveness. You begin to look through the lens of a new perspective and find understanding which brings lightness and love. By releasing stuck emotions from past experiences, whether it is shame, hurt, or guilt, we open ourselves to more awareness and acceptance. Breathe in and declare: *I take back my power. I am open, loving and confident.*

Now we move into the heart, which is the bridge between the upper and lower chakras. This is a moment where I'd like you to remember the image of the iceberg. All things below the surface impact the heart and can impact how we live our lives. We can show up as leaders in life or business, or not. The heart is our inner nurturer. This is where we give and receive from an *unconditional place*. When we are not yet free from experiences or wounds of the past, we are creating from a space that blocks the flow of the heart because we are afraid to give of ourselves. As we heal and open the pathways of the heart, we discover the flow, achieve grace, and feel at ease. Qualities of the heart are to be compassionate and caring, which can easily be given to others, but first, *we must give them to ourselves*. We can say, *I am love and I accept myself exactly as I am,* leading us to discover and open the receiving channels that confirm,

I deserve more love, happiness, and prosperity. Giving results from letting go of the conditions that prevented us from feeling free. Having healthy boundaries protects the heart. Giving is expressing who we truly are.

Are you able to give from the unconditional space from the heart, God's will or are you withholding because of the conditions set in place from past wounding? Pray to connect to the greatest love within you. The capacity of love is vast, and it is waiting for you.

The throat chakra is about communication. This is the place where we easily and freely speak our truth. As a woman, you may have experienced situations where you hold yourselves back. You want to have a conversation with your partner about life or money, but you hold back, to avoid speaking up because you fail to honor that what you have to say is important and see that it has value. It is those silent moments when we create imbalances and give power to underlying fears of not being approved of, the opinions of others, the fear of losing or not being liked, we choke the expression of our words. The shadow sides of our lower chakras prevent us from empowering ourselves at any moment. When we are in alignment, we are not seeking approval because we approve of ourself. We are free from those things that want to hold us back. We are free to express ourselves.

I encourage you to take back your power by speaking up and speaking out the moment you feel called to do so. Acknowledge that *I easily and effortlessly speak my truth.*

In the earlier years of my first marriage, I was shy and insecure. I wanted to speak up for myself, so I practiced speaking up and speaking out, which made me into the woman and public speaker I am today. To combat fears, I'd take in a full breath, ground myself, look upward, and ask for help. I would access the courage and guidance of my higher power at that moment, allowing me to express myself freely. I continue to build upon this muscle and in all things that require me to have more confidence. It is automatic because I trust that wisdom from within is given to me from a higher place and I trust the words I speak in the times I am asked to give a speech or guide a session with a client.

Moving into our third eye, we locate inner wisdom, visions, and intuition, being connected to and trusting in ourselves, as well as the guidance we receive through our intuition as messages from God. When we have a vision for ourselves, we don't get caught up in how it will work out. We trust and have faith that our higher power will guide us. What happens when we are called to do something in life, but we keep holding back because we fail to trust ourselves? We end up in a place of doubtful questioning, and soon we step into the shadow sides of ourselves.

Much like speaking up, power can come from pausing in silence, where we simply listen and avoid speech . In those moments when we choose to either pause or speak up because we are following internal guidance, we honor ourselves. Our voices and our souls are liberated to seek freedom of expression. When we play small, fear contracts us. When we speak out or pause, love has the opposite force as it expands us.

Women who don't know what they want in life or lack vision often have energy blockages in the lower chakra which prevent them from living life on their terms. Ask yourselves: *What fear or authority is preventing me from trusting myself?* Then we open the passageways to explore more of our potential. Yes, it may feel a little overwhelming. But as we know, the only way to eat an elephant is one bite at a time. Rather than eating elephants, we can practice being more grounded through journalling, yoga, and nature walks, whatever gives us a deeper connection to ourselves so we can begin living more of our truth in the present moment of the day we are in.

Which brings me to meditation. Many people say they have trouble meditating. I suggest playing with different types of meditation, perhaps trying a guided meditation, using a mantra, or taking off your shoes and walking barefoot on the grass to truly be with nature. Remember it is called a *mediation practice* for a reason. Pause to affirm, *I trust my inner wisdom.*

Moving up into our crown chakra, we find our connection to the divine. *Ask and receive. Between the asking and receiving are trust and patience.* with our pathways open, we are walking on our path with integrity. Say the words: *I am authentic. I show up. I'm enough just as I am at this moment.* The moments come when we find ourselves challenged, or we are in a state of fear, remember to say the words, *Help me out here. Protect me, guide me, help me find my way back to the center.* Asking in those moments helps us stand in our truth, and in those moments that we fail, it is okay because life is a journey of ebb and flow. Life will bring us plenty of growth opportunities.

Every moment provides an opportunity to grow in trust as we lean toward our strengths and gifts while moving through fears, allowing room to grow into abundance and integrate with the higher parts of ourselves. This is the process of the embodiment when we feel, *Beyond any doubt that yes, I am enough, it is completely safe to be me, I am deserving, and I love and value all parts of myself.*

In my experience, as I ended a cycle, I was tested about the resolve of who I am, and I was unshakeable because this is my truth and I feel it in my core.

Opportunities are filtered through the lens of our archetypal patterns. Knowing ourselves is a way to live in alignment. We are in alignment with the highest essence of who we are when we feel empowered, inspired, creative, and courageous. We are not in alignment when we feel insecure, doubtful, when we are hiding, or when we fail to trust. This is the duality that occurs within each of us, and it is a normal part of who we are. When we arrive in this place of duality, we practice by doing the work to move out of it more quickly, stopping the self-punishment patterns where we beat ourselves up. And as we grow in love, the tolerance of punishment is not a welcomed behavior.

I often say, *If we decide to eat the cake, eat it and enjoy it without the guilt, shame, or blame that usually follows the behavior we deem wrong or sinful.* It will be a pivotal day for us as we stand up and declare: *Enough! I will not beat myself up over this. I choose to love and accept myself exactly as I am.* The recurring mistake is when we keep beating ourselves up, inwardly punishing ourselves, thereby remaining trapped in self-sabotaging patterns and struggle. It is time to give our spirits grace and allow the energy in our bodies to flow with trust. Whether we are in an empowered, loving state or a disempowered, fearful state, we will vibrate at a higher or lower frequency.

In Louise Hay's book *You Can Heal Your Life*, she talks about how unexpressed emotions can create *dis-ease*. Our bodies will create diseases to communicate what our soul wants us to hear. Lower back issues are usually attributed to financial issues; inflexible knees are connected to relationships. In life, patterns of overspending, debt, money secrets, and spending to seek approval will show up and create dis-ease. These are symptoms of a deeper issue within our energy bodies that require clearing by doing deeper work. I do not claim to have all the answers for illness in the world. It is each individual soul lesson to explore their time on earth. Louise Hay's work has offered me some valuable guidance within my own body, and I have enjoyed learning from her perspective.

I listen to the energy in my body, and I allow it to be my guide. I trust that I am guided. When I make plans that do not always work out, it is okay. A healthy relationship would not give punishment for something that doesn't work out. I often do not care to set goals, and simply allow things to unfold naturally. Don't get me wrong, I do plan; however, I leave room for flexibility and non-attachment. When I receive an intuitive hit, I plan, then act and move forward to make it happen. Those are the plans that always work out for my highest good, even when I think they didn't, they did, and I will see the bigger picture after the fact in divine time.

Live Your Truth

My imprint that I lacked worth began at birth.

Looking back on the writing in my journal over the years, I recognize two common themes: God and money. Since I was a little girl, I prayed to God to someday make me happy. Being placed for adoption twice before the age of one, I was born into the energy of abandonment. My family did not know how to express love easily and love was what I've been seeking my entire life. My father took too much LSD in his twenties, triggering a schizophrenic mental illness that would prevent him from supporting our family mentally, emotionally, physically, or financially. I grew up in an environment of abuse, addiction, and violence. I did not grow up with a religious background; however, I do recall my grandfather being in the Salvation Army and on a couple of occasions attending Sunday school. My other grandfather was in AA over the years, which means he had some knowledge of a higher power. I am told by my aunt that I am most like him because of our shared gift of wisdom. For me, growing up in the presence of God was constant. I was in constant communication with God. When I became a mother,

I prayed for him to keep my children safe, happy, healthy, and normal every night.

It was God who answered my prayers and gave me the guidance to find my desires. *The Fulfillment of All Desires*, a book by Ralph Martin talks about our desires to be of God, meaning God gave us our desires and we get to use our will and free choice to follow the pathway to their unfolding. Again, my desires in life were clear: happiness, healthy relationships, and financial freedom.

Sitting on my deck in my country home, I realized I was living a dream come true. We had a total of sixty-nine acres. I had horses and dogs which I dreamt of having since I was a little girl. We hunted game on our very own property. This was a vision I had held for my life when I was younger, and I was living it. Yet, I still doubted and questioned my life. It was at that moment that I decided to trust completely, and I asked God to help me to let go of everything that was blocking the way. How could I keep questioning and regretting my life when it was clear my life had changed? Everything up to this point led me to this place. Some of my desires had been realized, but I was still seeking. I wasn't free yet.

It would take looking at the money relationship for me to find complete inner freedom and expand my connection with God. If you are a freedom seeker, I hope you find some meaning in my story.

Years ago, I read one of my favorite parables about God on a Harley. It was the story of God disguised as Joe,[3] a guy on a Harley. Joe would

---

3 Note: I use the name Joe in this story to protect the identity of men who were teachers in my life, men who showed up in personal relationships and financial matters.

show up in a woman's life to show her guidance along the way. Aren't we all potential guides to one another on our journey home? She had been longing for more in life and had yet to find it. She fell in love with Joe, which moved her toward a more fulfilling life.

As a young girl, I longed for someone to love me. As a teenager, I allowed myself to be used by boys hoping that this would give me the love I had been searching for. These behaviors only fueled my unhappiness and low self-esteem. I met my first husband at a local pub. We partied together and after only three months, I mentioned to a friend that I was going to break up with him. I didn't like him. However, I would remain with him for the next sixteen years because a week after I declared I was leaving, I found out I was pregnant. I was nineteen and figured it was meant to be. My marriage to him would not be a happy one and, it was a bit like living in a storm. I now know that no one else could make me happy because I was not happy within myself.

I was happy being a mother. Bringing my first daughter into the world was a defining and treasured moment in my life. With a full head of hair, she was placed on my chest. I found true love. My second child would be born less than two years later. Born prematurely, I believed at the time God was punishing me for my past behaviors. Later I learned that God never punishes me; I was the master of my self-punishment. Three years later, my third child came into the world. I never wanted to get married, however, after they were born, I figured it was time and the right thing to do. We got married in a small church in central Alberta.

---

https://www.psychiatrist.com/jcp/yoga-adjunctive-treatment-posttraumatic-stress-disorder/

I recall having dyed red hair and driving in an old Cutlass Supreme that was red with rust. At stop lights, I would have to keep my foot on the gas peddle and the break at the same time to keep it going. We celebrated with a few family members and friends in the basement of our townhouse. I borrowed my wedding dress from my neighbor. We were a young family, new from Newfoundland trying to make a living in Alberta. Like many traditional families, I was a stay-at-home mom. My husband's work took him away for two weeks and then he would spend time at home. I often enjoyed the times he was away more than when he was home.

Leaving Newfoundland had been a decision we made to save our relationship. Before moving, we went through a brief period of separation where I would hit rock bottom, only to return to the relationship I'd wanted to escape. I had no skills or courage to make it on my own. During our separation, for a short period, my two daughters were often cared for by their grandparents and a babysitter, while I worked and partied with friends. It was a horrible time in my life when my outer world reflected the truth of my inner world where I was drowning myself in bad habits. I was raped and only blamed myself as I put myself in the situation. If it weren't for being held in the arms of my girlfriends, I would have ended my life. I was powerless and returned to the relationship, where we moved to another province. Not much different from the women in my family, I was a young mom. I wanted things to be different, I just did not know how to change.

Sitting in a therapist's office, like I had so many times before, she asked me what I wanted. I said I want to be happy. Her reply was, to be happy you need to live your truth.

Live my truth.

That sounded easy, but I intuitively knew it would be hard. At that moment, a prayer I had prayed when I was five years old would be answered. *Dear God, please someday, make me happy.* I was willing and open to doing whatever it took to find happiness. Learning my truth was the first key given to me by God to find the way.

Teachers came into my life who would open the doorway to show me different healing modalities. We bought our first house in a small town where I met my first divine teacher. This woman had already awakened to herself and was living a conscious life. I enjoyed our deep, soulful discussions. She would answer my questions and then confront my behaviors by asking me questions to turn my attention inward, like the time she witnessed me yelling at my children.

She asked, "Why are you always yelling?"

I stopped to reflect why, "I don't know, everyone in my family yells." From that moment on, I became conscious of the times I was about to repeat the pattern, and I stopped. I began to communicate better. I went to Toastmasters, which helped me slow down and improve my pronunciation. She and I would read *The Dark Side of the Light Chasers* written by Debbie Ford. This helped me identify my emotional triggers, and I learned to take responsibility for myself by understanding the role of my emotions. I learned that *I could not control the actions of others; I could only control my actions.* The moments when I found myself emotionally triggered because of anger, jealousy, or resentment, I knew it was about me. I needed to look inside and ask myself, "Who am I and why am I acting this way." I finally recognized that I needed to acknowledge something deeper within myself to learn why I held emotions inside rather than releasing them or learning why they existed. The trigger was a clue: I needed to see and feel the emotion *at the moment* and then release it, freeing myself from acting out the pattern again. Becoming more conscious enabled me to do this. Being more conscious of my patterns gave me the ability to make new, empowered choices, versus staying stuck in old behaviors that trapped me in a cycle of unhappiness.

I began to practice speaking up for myself in my marriage. My entire life I struggled with shyness. I was the kid in school who would hide and think , *please do not pick me* when questions were asked. I lacked the confidence to speak up or speak out in most situations. My husband could be intense, and I experienced psychological abuse from him that frightened me. He never physically abused me; however, when I told him I wanted to leave the marriage on different occasions, his reactions were to stab a knife through a door with me on the other side or threaten my life with a shotgun. My responses to his reactions were always the same: I am sorry, why would I want to leave my family? There must be something wrong with me." He would back me up by saying, "of course, there is something wrong with you, look at your father." He knew I spent years crying over my father, and the times I spent with my father it was often violent and disruptive due to his mental illness. I stayed in this marriage because I was a child of divorce, and I never wanted my children to suffer as I did. Instead, I suffered, thinking this behavior was normal. He had a right to be angry or frustrated; however, any actions that threatened the life of another were not okay. This was the norm that I grew up with.

Being a battered woman can take many shapes. Battering is defined as a pattern of assaultive and controlling behaviors between adults in an intimate, sexual, theoretically peer, and usually cohabiting relationship. Battering occurs without regard for the victim's mental or physical well-being. It is done to punish, intimidate, control, and dominate. Resources are provided on my website www.janetkendrick.com that help to define battered women. I invite you to explore it and check any boxes that may relate to you, as it will tell you if you are involved in any form of intimate-partner violence. It is a form created by Jacqueline Aitken Kish at PACE Center, which is a community support center for trauma and sexual assault for women who needed black-and-white written answers that showed factual proof that they experienced some form of abuse. It is a tool that cannot be denied and lets them know the abuser requires help to change and the woman needs healing.

To break my pattern, I asked for help from God who gave me the courage to speak up and speak out. In those moments when I didn't speak up to avoid confrontation a little voice inside would say, *Janet, you have to say this*. I would turn around and muster the courage to speak up, finally breaking the pattern that had kept me trapped. I stopped denying the voice of the confident girl inside me. She was waiting to be free so that she could be heard. Her voice only needed to be cultivated with the grace of God. She would ask for help many times and he gave it every single time.

Next, I met a metaphysical healer who would open me up even more through our energy sessions. I rode horses with her and we met for weekly healing sessions. Being a girl from a small town in Newfoundland, I had no idea about healing or energy. I only knew I needed healing. I would lie on a table, where she would place her hands over me. Ro Hun therapy was a practice of looking at the shadow parts of self, the past hurts from experiences, and bringing the pain that had been stuffed inside to the surface for extraction. I began the process of healing my inner child and all the hurts I experienced at the hands of my father and a mother who did not know how to express love easily. I looked deeper to understand them. My father had grown up in an alcoholic environment. It had not been easy for him as the only boy of three girls. He was intelligent (some said genius), handsome, and he sang and played in a band. Then one weekend he would take too much LSD and was never the same again. He was often violent, and he beat my mother. On one occasion, he had been sleeping upstairs while my brother and I had been playing when we rolled on the bread mom had placed to rise by the heater. She woke him when she yelled at us. My brother and I must have been about five and three-and-a-half at the time. My dad roared down the stairs, sending us both to the room to wait for our beating with the belt. Terrified, we took the beating, but never told our father which one of us fell on the bread for fear we would get a more severe punishment. We were children, just playing. We certainly did not deserve this severity of punishment. My dad was a product of his environment, and he did not have the tools to control his anger or outbursts. Seeing how he grew up helped me to understand his reactions and I was able to forgive him for the things he did and for saying that I was not his daughter when I was an impressionable teenager, that I belonged to another man in town, along with the many other delusional things that were very confusing to a young girl. Looking at this through the lens of a new perspective, I could understand and even be empathetic towards my father. Forgiving him helped me let go of the pain I had held in my body for so long, and it opened my heart to love myself, and to acknowledge I was lovable. I was born enough, and I was finally able to discern the lies that made me feel otherwise.

My mother also grew up in poverty, violence, and alcoholic surroundings. Her father was a quiet man who showed little affection, perhaps because he had been raised by his uncles due to his mother's death at birth. Not having a mother to hold him or care for him no doubt resulted in a lack of emotional affection. My mother gave birth to me at the age of seventeen. Whether she did not want to take me home, or because she was told not to, at birth, I stayed in a hospital room for seven days with no contact from family. A nurse, out of pity and compassion , gave me my name Janet, which means *God is gracious* or a *gift from God*. I am unsure of all the details; however, a week had passed when my grandmother informed my mother that her father, my grandfather, said she could bring me home. She did, only to place me for adoption again three months later and this time it was to go to a family who lived down the road. My grandfather on my father's side denied that I was his son's child. My mother was out for a walk with me in a stroller and my grandfather had to stop for her to cross the road. He got out of his vehicle to look at me. The story told by my grandmother is that he came home and cried, as there was no denying, I was indeed his granddaughter. The adoption process would be stopped, and I would remain with my birth family.

During my sessions with this metaphysical healer, I began to see my mother through a different lens. I could see she loved me; she just could not show it in ways that I needed. Years later, a doorway would open to allow more love to be expressed between my mother and me. At the age of twenty-five, I called her with the full intention of hearing her tell me she loved me. I had healed enough at this point. I knew I was lovable, and it was time I heard it from my mother. After grounding and asking God to give me the courage to ask my mother, I called her on the phone and we had the following conversation:

"Mom, do you love me?"

"Of course I do, Janet. I am your mother."

A heavy silence filled the moment. "No Mom, I need to hear you say the words."

Silence, then. "*I love you, Janet. I am so proud of you.*"

In this moment, we broke the chains that locked our hearts. After that, we often spoke the words, *I love you.*

Union of Mind, Body, Soul

For most of my life, I longed for a relationship with God. I even thought about becoming a nun or going to Bible School to become a reverend. Inside, I felt a deep yearning that I wanted it more than anything else. I took Bible studies with Jehovah's Witness who willingly offered their time and, in my studies with them, I had hoped to find this connection.

I do not think a day has gone by without my being in constant communication with this elusive guide I always called God. Later, from a Christian perspective, I could see Jesus as a pathway to God; however, I already had direct communication with him and believed that, in healing, we could be more like Christ as we grow in consciousness. There lies the foundation of my practice: to be more like Christ in healing and sharing my wisdom while being a presence of love. I do receive peace when I read the Bible daily and enjoy the messages while keeping my mind open to expanding its perception of my relationship with God. A friend once admitted they felt I had a direct line to God, as they witnessed my receiving miracles on more than one occasion. I was baptized as a Christian and feel my beliefs are more universal. I am a child of God and feel strong in my spirituality as I love him with all my mind, heart, and soul.

A friend introduced me to yoga in my mid-twenties during the beginning of my healing journey. When I first sat on the mat in a gymnasium, I was home. Later, I recognized that I did not need to go to church to find God and Yoga would deepen this connection. Yoga is the union of the mind, body, and soul. It was the space I found on the mat that allowed me to stay quiet and listen to the soft inner voice inside. The practice of Asanas which are movements in postures that strengthened and toned my body. It also helped me release tension stress, and stuck emotions from my body, allowing me to renew on a deeper level.

An article from the Journal of Clinical Psychiatry[4] shows yoga as an adjunctive treatment for post-traumatic stress disorder. In trial studies, yoga significantly reduced PTSD symptomatology and yoga may improve the functioning of traumatized individuals by helping them tolerate physical and sensory experiences associated with fear and helplessness, increase emotional awareness and build tolerance.

This study also connected the dots for me and my experience with yoga and healing. I discovered how to deepen my breathing to shift from shallow breathing and living to deeper breathing and living life more fully. In my mediation, the space between my thoughts was mere seconds in the beginning, evolving to more space and greater pockets of peace from the usual mind chatter. Yoga began the process of coming

---

4 https://www.psychiatrist.com/jcp/yoga-adjunctive-treatment-posttraumatic-stress-disorder/

home to myself uniting with God and finding freedom within because I would hear my truths as He whispered the ways for me to follow.

When I got baptized at People's Church as a Christian while standing outside in the communal area, the drops of water falling upon my head felt like an intuitive sensation. This feeling was strange yet real. I remained open to the experiences of energy on many different levels from then on. Yoga took me beyond my body to the receiving spirit. The quieter I became the more I felt an increase in energy and a growth in intuition. I began to let go of living lies and listen closer to my truth.

Intuition is said to be God's way of communicating with us. The inner knowingness is the feeling of sensation or witnessing energy within our body that resonates as truth within us. Helping me see what is right for me through connection with feelings. Yoga for me is a pathway to God and finding myself. Through a process of releasing and opening, we begin to receive his spirit or open the connection to hearing the messages of our inner guide. *Getting grounded in who we are inside changes how we are on the outside as a result of letting go of a false perception that you may have been living because of imprints placed on you by another or from life's experiences.* Maturation is the awareness of who you are and who you are becoming by letting go of what is no longer yours to keep in this present moment.

I had a kundalini experience with my second husband. He was the first man that I trusted and felt safe with. He helped me change my foundation and I began to grow new roots as a result of this safety. A surge of electrical energy raced from the base of my spine to the top of my head when we engaged in intimacy at the beginning of our relationship. It was also with him that I created my first contract with financial independence, which was especially important to me after my first marriage ended. I asked him if he would be okay managing his money and I would manage mine. Keeping our accounts separate, we agreed never to tell each other what to do regarding money. I mention money here hoping you will eventually see the thread of how we are with money and the way it plays into other areas of our lives. How we act in our money relationships can reveal patterns or behaviors in others. Everything is connected. As I look back over my life, I can see how all the pieces of the puzzle fit my matrix.

When I began teaching yoga I felt an energy shift. Teaching was very natural for me and my energy increased as it moved through me, and I heard my inner voice more clearly. People often refer to intuition as an inner voice and when you learn to trust it, that voice inside gets bigger and louder, and the clear choice is to listen. I recall feeling an entirely different kind of energy for the first time when my aunt took me to visit my father at a mental institution. I was twelve. I can still feel the energy I felt in the air on that day as I walked into that building. It was heavy and dense, like walking into a thick fog. I cried for days after the experience. My sensation with energy is the opposite of that experience when I teach. From the very beginning as a yoga teacher, I felt an energy being expressed through me. Over time and with experience, I learned that I could always trust it to be there for me. I would ask for guidance from the spirit, and it would always be there in circumstances when I needed courage in a conversation to speak up or with help in teaching a class.

Teaching yoga has given me a sense of living *on purpose*. It feels easy and natural for me. During the first years following my first divorce, when I did not see two of my daughters for three years and my youngest only stayed with me on weekends, I taught yoga four nights a week and worked a full-time job. I was in survival mode, and I often found myself surrendering on the mat, preparing to teach exhausted mentally and emotionally. I would look up and say, *You've got this*. I trusted the spirit to work through me and teach the class, and on many occasions, the spirit carried me when I could hardly carry myself. I was always in awe of and grateful thinking about who or what was being expressed through me at the times I was teaching class. It was me, and I was full of body and spirit.

When I first left the banking world to begin working in the insurance industry, it opened me up to creativity I did not know existed. I was inspired to teach women about money and how to achieve their financial independence. Downloaded information came through me in mediation where I created workshops and developed content for newsletters. Everything flowed with grace and ease. I recall thinking this is what it must be like to be a channeler of energy. It also signifies the moments I accessed more of my brain's capacity as I received insights into talents I never knew existed. This was a balancing of my chakras from my root to my crown.

I am extremely grateful for my time in the banking world. It opened me up to learning about money management on a physical level. I also got to learn that I was smart enough since in my youth, math was not my strong suit. In grade ten I half completed a math exam where I got ten percent, failing because I didn't complete the exam and feeling not so smart with numbers or the concepts. In my work I realized that I was always smart enough, I just had bigger challenges in life to deal with at that time. I always had a curiosity for learning and enjoyed learning about investments, and other aspects of money management. I got to discover other things about myself too such as my deep sense of shame around the bankruptcy that occurred after my first marriage. I was also emotionally sensitive to people and their energy however I did not have an understanding about just how sensitive I was at that time. I had a regular yoga practice at that time which helped me to be grounded however if I worked with estate matters or too many people with negative energy, I would find myself overly emotional and would have to close my office door to cry.

A good friend who knew I felt emotions on a deep level advised me to practice grounding often and to wash my hands in between client meetings. This practice helped me in my grounding and getting a better balance in my emotions. It was my love for working with people and curiosity to learn about money that led me into the banking world, along with my desire for financial freedom. After three years of working in the bank, I was ready to enter another level in my life. I began to listen to my inner voice which encouraged me to take a risk and enter the entrepreneurial world. My inner voice asked, *If not now, when?* I started exploring my options to leave the banking industry for the insurance world, in search of achieving my desires for more time and freedom–financial freedom. The newness of energy, creativity, and inspiration confirmed I was on the right path. I was aligned and entering a new field where I could feel energy transmit from myself to others that I met. It was inspiring and fulfilling as I opened to receive greater possibilities.

Wayne Dyer talks about this field of energy in his book *The Power of Intention,* quoting researchers who believed that our intelligence, creativity, and imagination interact with the energy field of intention rather than being thoughts or elements in our brain. Dyer referenced the brilliant scientist, David Bohm, author of *Wholeness and the Implicate Order*, who wrote that all ordering influence and information is present in an invisible domain or higher reality and can be called upon in times of need. I felt this when I called out for help and would feel the intelligence as a guide from inside or perhaps above. Lynne McTaggart shows scientific studies in her book *The Field: The Quest for the Secret Force of the Universe* supporting the existence of a higher, faster energy dimension of the field of intention that can be tapped into and used by anyone. The energy that the other writers talked about is one I kept opening up to that revealed more things about myself. This sense of intelligence that moved through me became easier to access. Whether I was teaching a yoga class, designing a workshop, or preparing a speech, I would tap into this field of intention and allow it to reveal through me the creativity, and ideals needed to be heard in the moment. On one occasion I was asked to speak at a ladies' lunch which would happen the next day at noon. I excitedly agreed to the opportunity to speak, and the next morning, as I sat in meditation the topic came to me. I felt confident in the message which was to discuss what a woman's greatest asset in business was and myself to deliver the information that came through me. I trust it to always be there for me and all times when I need it. It's a powerful presence to be felt and work with. I began to strengthen and open the pathways so at times when I needed help, I looked up to ask, and I would receive the guidance instantly. This intelligence, which I know as God also made sense when I heard it spoken in the Course of Miracles, which is a guide on spiritual living based on universal principles with its roots in Christianity. The holy spirit, intelligence, universe, and divine are the inner guidance systems within each of us to return us to God. In my search for God, it was love that I wanted most, please someone to love me. As I found love within myself, what was not love, fell out of my life and I found myself even closer to God. I began to live God's will as I expressed my gifts and talents and let go of the ways of the world and finding the freedom that this offered. This gave me a deeper sense of grace and patience in my life. The striving and searching had ended because I found what I had been seeking. God and Love. It was learning about the energy of money and sacred money archetypes that I would learn more in order to deepen this connection.

Yoga took me on a journey of self-knowledge toward understanding myself. My efforts at emotional mastery prepared the way for me to open more to the field of intention and intelligence as I learned the dance of my energy through my emotions. Yoga is a practice I have done daily since I was first introduced to it in my twenties. The practice also keeps me in excellent health and youthful , as people often tell me I keep getting younger, and I'm certain I will age gracefully because of my yoga practice.

The Energy of Fear

My husband and I spent our last vacation together in Cayo Coco, an island in Cuba during February of 2020 . When we arrived home, we heard the news of the pandemic. I registered my business as Prosperous Woman Financial Coach in March of 2020 and I operated in both the insurance and coaching world before I made the full shift into my business. There was an energy of fear that I felt in the air that compelled me to go deeper. It started the moment I went to the grocery store; the energy had a similar resonance as the day I visited my father in the mental institution, I felt the heavy thickness of fear in the air.

I walked out to face my husband who had been waiting in the truck. He saw the tears streaming down my face and asked, "Are you okay?"

"Yes," I answered. "let's go home. I felt a deep need to go inward."

The first book I took off my shelf was Caroline Myss, *Entering the Castle, Finding the Inner Path to God and Your Soul's Purpose*. I was on my way to receiving the connection I had been seeking my entire life. Little did I know, by fall I would experience it completely. Not long after Myss' book I was attracted to Kendal Summerhawk, a woman who could have been an older version of myself. She was a wealthy woman who had a love of horses. I felt drawn to take her certification in archetypes. Once certified, my first student was a friend, TEDx speaker, coach, and author Candace McKim whom I had known while living in Grande Prairie. Candace was a long-time friend, yogi, and author of the book, *Intuition is a Choice*. She also helped me name my business when, the previous fall I volunteered to help her at a speaking event on Women, Wealth, and Worth. I mentioned I needed a title for an article I'd written that was being featured in a local Synergy Magazine. Being an intuitive woman, she announced, "I see Prosperous Woman." Which naturally led to the birth of my coaching business in the months that followed.

I guided Candace through the archetypal journey where she uncovered deeper hidden beliefs, like "Who do you think you are?" Being a ruler archetype like me, Candace had a high drive for success that she also felt negative about. She started to embrace more grace on her journey as she cultivated her natural talents. She then took a big leap to work with David Beyers's coaching program. Candace continues to excel in her career as a leader for women in business connecting with the power of intuition and is the founder of Intuitive Coaching Academy where she trains spirited entrepreneurs and women how to access and use these inherited gifts in life and business. She and I are connected on this journey, and when I think of her, she always reaches out. I consider her a soul sister and trusted wise friend.

My next student would be another dear friend who came to me because she was struggling. She had always been a spiritual woman but was feeling lost and disconnected from her spiritual roots. She had been an accumulator archetype and needed to embrace more respect and appreciation for herself, she came to me as she had been struggling for some time and was seeking guidance. She had wounds from a past relationship that needed healing, and being a nurturer archetype, she was great at giving to others but failed at giving herself what she needed. Her inner tank was empty, and she agreed she needed to create time for herself to do this work as she was fearing the worst and depression was at a high. The initial investment was difficult for her, however, spending money on others was an easy choice to make, however, I told her that investing in herself would lead to her feeling empowered. What she had been doing wasn't working, and she was desperate for a change and was ready to go deeper. At the beginning of every session, I would do a chakra cleansing and grounded mediation to ensure we were both connected. I evoked the presence of God and her guides, then we went to work. One day, when I added in reiki work, she expressed how she felt energy melting from her body, like mud pouring out from her skin. She felt she had spiritual healing and began feeling renewed and whole and as she made shifts in her inner world the struggle on the outside began to loosen its grip. She had renewed her strength and began her spiritual practices once again, deepening her relationship with God that she had lost sight of over the years.

The emotions that are felt when individuals take the sacred money archetype assessment are everything from feeling fearful and curious to excited. I know that many people have resistance and fears when it comes to money, including me on many occasions throughout my life. One man cried about all the pressure he felt around supporting his family. We did not work together but the reading alone opened a pathway for him by helping him understand himself more which provided the relief he needed in letting go of some of the pressures he had been feeling. Another man completed the assessment and felt so much fear that it took ten minutes for him to make his computer work. After his reading, he mentioned his resistance to hearing about archetypes and felt relieved to discover he was more in alignment with his life than he had realized and could see the challenges that he had worked through. The energy of fear would be evident in technology as static or interruption of images on my computer and when individuals would show up in a Zoom meeting it would take several minutes for audio or video to work properly. I've seen it often and simply waited patiently for it to pass when meeting with people for their archetypal readings. In the delay, they always stated how much resistance they had been experiencing before our meeting. I have learned to hold space for fear, and I can also see my moments where I failed to recognize fear in dealing with those I cared for which led to the disruption of relationships. Fear, along with resentment, hate, judgment, and criticism will create separation within ourselves and our relationships.

David R. Hawkins MD, Ph.D. talks about the energy of fear in his book *The Map of Consciousness*. His years of studies proved the frequencies of energy in all things. Feelings of fear, guilt, shame, blame, and grief are on a lower frequency vibration, and trust, willingness, optimism, peace, joy, and love are higher in vibration. His book uses the energy scale to help people actualize their ultimate potential.

My energy was divided between my insurance business and coaching, and I felt the moment when I needed to make a choice, as it was too much to do both. There was so much to learn about in either world. While considering my choices, I received a call from a former co-worker from RBC who asked if I would consider partnering as an IRP, a retirement investment specialist. Given everything that was going on in the world and the pandemic, I said I would be open to considering the possibilities. I was drawn to coaching and sat down to type a letter to the insurance brokerage I was working with at the time. When I put my hands on the keyboard, I realized I should tell my husband about my decision first. He immediately walked in the door; I met him in the kitchen.

I said, "I wanted to let you know, I am letting go of the insurance work to focus on my coaching business." He was about to say something, but I stopped him. "I am not asking for your opinion; I am simply letting you know." I walked back into my office and emailed the letter.

It was a profound moment for me. It was the first time in my life that I approved of myself rather than seeking the approval of another person. This defining moment felt like an important change in my life. However, I did resume my consideration of the banking offer and had several meetings with RBC. My husband encouraged me to consider the offer, especially because of the times. I said I would at least take the course required for the role. I completed the test and failed. My heart was not in it. Yes, it guaranteed a salary for six months but after that, I'd go on full commissions. It didn't make a lot of sense to me as I was currently in a commission role working for myself. I wanted to give myself a chance to follow my heart and what I felt I had been led to do.

At one point my husband had been away on a trip in British Columbia. During a phone conversation, he said, "You better take that job."

I heard my inner voice say, "I'll leave if he forces my hand." This was the moment I unknowingly set an intention that would begin our separation. I declined the bank offer and went to work on my business. When my husband returned from his trip, he said "I hope you are successful, but I do not support you, and you must immediately begin paying twenty-five hundred dollars a month to the mortgage." I stubbornly agreed. Until this point in our marriage, my husband had paid for the household expenses. I would contribute by sharing the cost of vacations and portions of renovations that needed to be done. One of my motivating factors for wanting to earn and create more money was to be an equal contributor. I had an audacious goal of paying off his mortgage as a way of saying thank you to him for being the main provider. On my dream board, I wrote: Be mortgage-free by June of 2023 . On that exact date, I joked with a friend as I was homeless and between moves. It was another reminder for me to be careful and clear about what I ask for in life.

I went to work on my business and I was completely in love with my life. I had an assistant and an editor, and our team flowed together. Within three months I showed my husband my tracking sheet of income and I had cleared what I would have grossed at the bank. His response was silence. He had nothing to say. Shortly after that, I mentioned I felt a separation between us.

His response was, "You're going to leave me." He added whenever a woman says that it means she is getting ready to leave." I was his third wife, and he was reacting from a fearful place. I did not say that to him, I simply witnessed his reaction and assured him that I was not going to leave him. I had no intention of leaving my marriage ever. December came, and I fell short on my mortgage payment because I'd hired a coach which caused me to overextend myself financially. Otherwise, I would have made the mortgage payment. I had a habit of spending beyond my means and made the impulse to hire her because I felt it would help me in becoming more successful faster. His response as he sat on the steps in my office was, "As your business manager, I get to tell you what to do."

I listened to his words and inside, I raged. I tried to explain. "It's not always realistic to meet income targets when you are new in the business," and asked for some flexibility. I tried to make him see that asking for me to meet this payment amount was unrealistic and he wasn't being fair. I was manipulated in the beginning when he requested that amount because I chose to do my business and not take the bank position, but he refused to hear me or understand my explanation. He was rigid and stood firm about the situation, telling me it was my fault and responsibility. The bank would not care about my reasons for not making a mortgage payment only that I was delinquent on my payment. I went for a drive and called a girlfriend to vent my frustrations. I had been triggered and I knew it when these words came out of my mouth, *"No man will tell me what to do, ever."*

In April of the following year, our family and friends gathered around a fire one evening. My daughter-in-law had just lost her father and was asking some deeper questions about our souls when my husband took it upon himself to interrupt our conversation and loudly made a point to disrespect and devalue my spiritual beliefs stating there was no real God. The next day, I told him, "I want to share my life with you, except there is a separation happening between us."

Once again, his response was, "You are going to leave. That's it. I am getting a lawyer and filing for a divorce."

"No," I assured him, "I am not leaving you. I only want to share my life with you. I want to share the work I am doing. It matters to me. I believe that fear will create a division not only within us, but it will also push love out of our relationships as well."

The following month, three days before Mother's Day, I had an unusual feeling in my heart. It was noticeable but unidentifiable. I began seeing repeating numbers such as 333 which translated to relationships and letting go. I had a strange interaction with a girl who responded negatively to what I had said, and I witnessed her reaction. It was early morning when I sat at my computer to meet another woman for the first time over a Zoom meeting. She was a well-known healer and when I opened my computer, my screen went white. Files and messages were popping up all over my screen and nothing I did could control it. I asked her if she could see what was happening. I wondered if the message was for her, but she said, "It is happening to you, not me." What happened next was shocking. A pdf file from Denise Thomas Duffield, who authored several books around money and wealth popped open on my screen. It read, *"Do it now lucky bitch."*

Next, was the evening before Mother's Day, my middle daughter came to visit. As she walked towards me, I immediately burst into tears. She hugged me and asked me what was wrong.

The words burst out of me. "I feel this wound in my heart, it's about your father and my husband. It needs healing."

The next day, again spontaneous tears erupted from me in a conversation with my mother-in-law, I excused myself from our conversation explaining that I was feeling emotional. She assured me that it was okay. We were preparing a fire outside for a morning brunch before the family arrived. One look at my face, and my husband immediately stopped to ask me what was wrong. Again, these words burst out of my mouth, "Something is going on between us. I don't like it and it must stop now."

He stopped. Then he said, "I don't like you. I blame you. I resent you because I am going to have to work until I am seventy years old. You are not the woman I married." He continued to vent all the feelings he had stored inside for the past year. I sat in silence and listened. He needed to get it all out, so I simply remained open to hear the feelings he'd held on to for far too long. Then our family arrived, and we went about our day as if nothing had happened. The next day, I approached him to have a conversation. This was a big deal and we had more to discuss. He was busy and focused on his tasks for the day, and his response was, "We're good. There is nothing to talk about."

I went for a walk and received this intuitive message. "You need to leave." I looked up to God and asked him, "You want me to leave?" The words were loud and clear.

I returned home and saddled my horse. Right before leading my horse into the riding arena, my phone opened to a conversation about people pleasing from the girl I had a negative experience with earlier in the week. I got on my horse. I could sense something was unfolding around my life. My stepson and his girlfriend arrived to drop off their dog, which they did each time they went to do some activity. They were unable to keep the dog in their apartment and kept lying to the property owner about having the dog. I was immediately triggered.

I knew it was about me. I looked inside myself and asked, "What is it that I need to see here or let go of?" Immediately a vortex of energy moved from head to toe washing the energy of lies through me. I got off my horse, unsaddled her, and put her in her stall.

I met my husband in the kitchen. I confronted him, "We need to talk."

He stood across from me, separated by the island in the kitchen. He repeated what he'd said previously. "I don't like you. You are not the woman I married. I want my old wife back. I resent you and I blame you. You need to leave."

I walked upstairs, packed a bag, and left. I called my girlfriend along the way to ensure I had a place to stay while I found a place of my own. She welcomed me. Later in the week, I had the instinct to call a previous client to ask if she had a place for rent. I had no idea if she did, I just followed my intuitive hit. She did have a place. She had an empty trailer on an acre of land. It was an hour out of town. The internet was not great, which was a concern since my business was online. She allowed me to stay for a few days to feel it out. The place was beautiful and was surrounded by golden wheat fields. I lay on the grass and felt completely safe and secure. I had little money, no furniture, and a single mattress to sleep on. I knew I was protected and being divinely guided. Surrounded by wheat fields, I opened my arms wide. I felt wide open.

I looked for an apartment in town that would allow my dog and found a basement suite where I spent four days. The noise upstairs kept me up until four in the morning and I cried. This was not for me.

I spoke with my husband. He agreed to counseling and I could move home. Waiting for the counselor, three minutes before she came on, he declared he could not do this and walked out. When the counselor arrived, she encouraged me to acknowledge my feelings as they had value.

Later my husband and I sat together outside. He assured me that he was not changing. He asked if I could accept that. I spoke no words as I knew the energy between us had already been divided. We had sex twice when I returned home and my organism had been sharp, not releasing, which told me we were ending.

Shortly after, I received a call from Scotiabank making me an offer to work there. I stated, "You must have the wrong person. I did not apply for a position with you."

My husband said it was a gift and I should consider it, that maybe it would save our marriage. I took the job, and on each of the four days

I was there, I knew I did not belong. I cried from the depths of my soul during my lunchtime walks. I then received a call from my former branch manager at RBC. He heard where I was working and said, you belong here. Because I had a previous relationship with them, I would consider the offer. It was my out.

After giving my notice at Scotiabank, I felt a strong need to leave town to get clear within myself. And my husband and I needed space away from each other.

My girlfriend had moved to the mountains in British Columbia. She agreed I could spend as much time as I needed. The drive was thirteen hours. At about the halfway mark, I began to feel clearer. I asked myself if I wanted to return to RBC. The answer was a resounding no. I pulled over, emailed the manager, and graciously declined his offer. My husband called shortly after to notify me that he was filing for a divorce and that our marriage was over. All along, everything was unfolding for the greater good, driven by the higher consciousness of my life. I permitted myself to not make any decisions about where I would live. I needed time and that is exactly what I gave myself. I asked my girlfriend and her husband if I could live in their holiday trailer in exchange for rent and I would also help with cleaning the suites of her Airbnb.

I felt happy inside. I did yoga, meditated daily, walked, and spent time working as a housekeeper. I allowed myself to cry whenever the emotions surfaced. Over time, it was intuition that would lead me to stay as the energy of the town felt harmonious. Standing on the property

I would later rent; I remembered a dream I had a year prior about flying through a valley of mountains and another one of me flying over a mountain that was straight across the top. I looked around. I was in the exact mountain that was in my dream and the property sat between a valley of mountains.

The Energy of Love

My entire life I searched the earth for someone to love me. I did not find it in another individual. I found it within myself. My next partner (I'll call him Joe) mirrored for me what the love in me could no longer tolerate in a relationship. At the same time, his amazing energy removed what no longer belonged in me and brought a deeper healing and wholeness. The lesson would not be easy. After two years, Joe would impact me like no one did before and it left me stripped bare, in search of a deeper understanding of the experience I had with him.

Joe appeared a couple of months after I decided to live in the little mountainous town. Before meeting him, I felt my energy reach outward, searching and I immediately pulled it back and declared "No way. I am not ready." When I heard his voice for the first time, I thought he sounded like a nice guy, which was the same thing I'd said about my husband. When I received a text message from Joe that was very playful, it made me curious to know more about this guy. Meeting him for the first time, there was an instant electrical current between our left eyes. He immediately looked away. I felt the spark.

I knew I was meant to meet this guy, but I was not ready. I still had grieving to do. So, I continued to grieve. One day several months later, I woke up and felt I had released my husband. I had the sensation that I had stepped over a line, ready to let go and leave us behind. I stood at the top of my stairs and announced to the Universe, *"Show me a prosperous life!"*

In that same instant, Joe called. I felt a rush of energy run through my root chakra. It was time. I would learn that he was a conscious man by the words he spoke, that he mentioned how he willed things into his life. He also asked a lot of questions and we discovered we had much in common. Joe would challenge me to go deeper, to claim my value and worth, and send me seeking to heal inside so that I would never attract an unhealthy relationship again with a partner. This meant I needed to get clear about who I was, what I wanted in life, and whether I was willing to do what it took to reach my dreams. Did I have what it would take to live in alignment and maintain it to achieve something better or to be better?

You won't get very far on your journey with one foot on the ship and one foot on the shore. (Author Unknown) The wisdom to me in this quote is we can have one foot in both worlds, that we are divided within ourselves until we are no longer divided. Love or fear, and everything else in between is perception which can change as our stories change and we heal.

First, we would need to strip it all down.

I could share this part of my story from the lens of a woman who was emotionally and psychologically abused. I could say, I was subjected to narcissism, gaslighting, and love bombing.

I could share that I was a woman with deeper abandonment issues, and because of unhealed wounds, I was triggered by someone else's boundaries.

I could also share that the individuals in my story also had wounds, and potentially their boundaries were healthy and rigid, based on their own stories and lived experiences.

I could also say that I am empathic, which makes me sensitive to the emotions of others, and that I can pick up on toxic traits as a result of reaching higher levels of love and cleaning out my negative traits. I feel energy, I am sensitive to the changes in the moon cycle as well as the energy of others. I am a person who takes responsibility and accountability, and I will take things to heart if you are too harsh with your words. I feel their power. Words can lift us or tear us down. Which words are you choosing to speak to yourself and others?

I could also say, too often, because of my hidden fears, and people-pleasing qualities that I have avoided putting important boundaries in place, however for years, I had been learning how to do just that, become healthier, and more whole so that I could be happier.

The point I am trying to make is that we all view life through a lens that is filtered through our stories of past experiences. Some good and some bad, yet they all make up our perception. Truth is malleable, as what is my truth may not be yours. I cannot argue with you about what you feel is right or wrong; who am I to tell you what you need to do to live your life? And the same goes for me, taking care of me, is my role, so that I can be better in me, which may or may not have benefits to you. If I take care of my well-being, then I can be better. What if, rather than bringing our judgment, criticism, or lack of love, to the ring, we bring an openness, a willingness to hear and understand one another?

How would it feel if we talked, allowed room for our differences, and healthy conflict? What if, I saw the value in you and you saw the value in me, and we cared about one another's highest good? What if, we strived to use our power for good and agreed that we would each work on our own egos or dark parts of self so that we could all feel safe and loved? What if, we agreed that our experiences shaped our beliefs and patterns, and we could change if we wanted to if it meant we would each as a result of doing that work bring more love to the table?

That would be a new kind of ecosystem to our culture. One that says we all matter and from the time we came into the world we were born enough and were already loved. Now from that place of love, go out into the world and breathe more love.

Joe has an advocate or spirit within, he has both light and darkness. I have witnessed him work through his darkness to find understanding, and a solution to find peace. I also witnessed him deny his darkness and I mine. He is a human who cares for animals and others, and he too is sensitive to others and strives to live life in love, and alignment. Like me, he follows his internal guidance to live life to the fullest and be happy.

To look at the narcissist in Joe meant I needed to look at my narcissism. On a conscious level, we are all one. Meaning all the qualities within you are in me.

I read a paper written by M.D. Rankel on May 22, 1996, her writings resonated with my thinking and explanations of my story. I would like to share that her piece talked about three philosophers and scientists, Dr. K. Dabrowski, Rudolph Steiner, and G.I. Gurdjieff, whose writing talked about consciousness, transformation, and freedom. It stated that each of these men claimed that man, as he is, is in the process of becoming human and that, as individuals, we have exceeded to a greater or lesser degree. They all agree that man is unconscious, at worst an animal, and at best a machine, and that he must first awaken and realize that this is the case. Then he must work to try hard not to go back to sleep. Each writer tried to provide a roadmap that would guide others through uncharted territory to the higher world of human experience. I find it fascinating, and yet it was mentioned that no one thought like me. I am not unique in my thinking; my thinking is just different. However, I too am sharing a roadmap to get to your truth, so that you can transcend what is below to above and find your freedom.

In my eyes, Joe lived a higher human experience. He used his powers for good, until me, which at times he misused his powers. I also misused mine, as I did not stand in my power. Joe asked me to be honest, to not live in fear. He stated that I did not even know my power. He encouraged me to stand on my own two feet, to know myself. At his core, freedom was most important, and it was easier to be single than to settle into a partnership that wasn't in alignment.

He asked me to grow up and see my higher self. The thing is, he too needed to grow up. We all do. Joe had behaviors triggered fear in me because I had wounds from my past experiences. The lesson that I would learn challenged me, I would run in fear several times, which was also my body's natural stress response. My nervous system was triggered by all the changes in my life, based on the choices that I made. I had reached a high place of love within myself, and then my husband of twelve years, whom I gave all of myself to and sacrificed for, only to have him rip me out of his life like a bandage, with no communication only the warnings I felt in my body leading up to the situation. Inside over the years, I was motivated by love to be and do better, but I was also motivated by fear, I wanted to prove to him that I could be an equal contributor, that he mattered, and that I wanted what was best for everyone, yet I created pain, and I was selfish on my healing journey. In the end, I could understand why he acted the way he did, and why it was easier for him to rid himself of a woman who was independent and didn't need him. That all of my changing, scared him, and my conversations made him feel uncomfortable. He has years of practice protecting his emotions because of his career. It was easier to compartmentalize than feel the things he had to witness. As a father who fought to have custody of his children, it was okay for me to be without mine and he wasn't willing to support me in my fight but wait he did support me. He provided a home and took care of the finances. He did the best he could do at the time, or maybe he didn't. Could he have done better? Of course, including me, we all can. Intimacy is into you; I can see me. How do we feel about one another, we both have something to learn, wouldn't you agree? Do we feel safe with one another? Can I trust you, am I too trusting? There is so much here to unpack, and what I am expressing can feel overwhelming. Life can be like that, but what if, we were grounded in who we are, love, and cultivated a culture where we feel enough, that it is safe to be heard, and sometimes we hurt, yet we have value and worth and we cared, practice more empathy. Would it change how you lived your life? Would it change the world? I like to think so. What if the currency of money changed, how would that change our lives? What would we be in pursuit of then? For whom would we live?

There is a quote by Maya Angelo, that when we know better, we do better. That is true, but sometimes we know better and don't do better because we step back into old patterns or have beliefs and values that support us differently at various times of our lives.

Joe was the first higher-level conscious male relationship I entered, one that mirrored what I needed to let go of and what I needed to embrace more of. He helped me become clear about what needed to be released from all past relationships and begin the healing of my inner child's wounds. With him, my patterns and those of many generations of women before me would be cleared once and for all. It was based on an unhealthy dependence on unhealthy men.

Joe spent the first few days listening to me and he was very interested in what I had to say. I shared with him how I felt I had arrived at the height of myself spiritually. He just laughed. At the time, I did not know how conscious he was. He had been in a relationship, so we did not cross any lines, only talked. By the third day, I desired him. I could tell by the look on his face that he too was struggling with an inward battle and that he also desired me. When I told him how I felt, he said he was another girl's man. I simply said, well you go figure that out and if things don't work out, you know how I feel. He left, stopping at the end of his driveway. Inside, he acknowledged he did not want to be without me, yet he had to go. The next time I saw him, he greeted me with a kiss and said, "Now I'm available."

You would never tell the shape of Joe by the clothes that he wore. Most often it was a pair of blue bibbed coveralls. When I went to watch a movie with him at his place, and I saw his perfectly round ass covered in red briefs, I was instantly impressed. This man was in great physical shape. When he first entered me, I gasped. He was perfect. When he kissed me, it was as if he sucked my breath from me. In bed, we intertwined our arms, legs, and body. We were identical in height, and when he took the archetype assessment, we were identical in our top two as ruler and maverick. This man was the definition of abundance in all aspects of his life.

I truly felt we were gifts to each other. Sexually, I felt safe with him. I was open to exploring new sensual territory. I'd had the same style of sex for the past twelve years. There was nothing vanilla about my playtime with Joe. I allowed him to dominate me, out of curiosity yet it also confused me, and I wondered if letting him have that much power over me was a good thing.

One day, I mentioned in a text that some guy had hit on me while I was standing in line. He was upset and asked if I needed that kind of attention. No, I only mentioned it and I don't need attention from another man. I quickly discovered he had extremely high expectations that were loaded with disappointments. When I left his house one morning, I did not put away the coffee. He told me he wouldn't tolerate me not picking up after myself. Joe had built an empire where everyone did their part, which meant he did not have to pull their weight too. He believed and practiced that it is the responsibility of many to build a successful company or relationship.

We had an open discussion about money and let me know he would appreciate not always fronting the bill and that he would like it if I bought him coffee once in and while. I was appreciative of our conversations and would give where and when I could in plenty of small ways. When he felt I was not contributing enough he would let me know. I mentioned one day that I purchased a punch pass for a sound bath for two hundred dollars. He pulled to the side of the road to remind me, "You were not an equal contributor in your marriage which didn't feel good for your ex-husband." He then questioned my spending on such a frivolous item.

My heart sank and I felt so guilty. I cried, reliving how wrong I had felt in my past relationship. I did not want to repeat that pattern. He was also an accumulator archetype and money spent on sound baths, reiki, or things such as massage seemed like luxury items to him. To me, they were a was a common, self-caring part of my life. It was what I valued.

It didn't take long for me to discover he did not like my celebrity archetype. It reminded him of his ex-wife, and he felt celebrities were attention seekers. He announced his displeasure with other spiritual workers in my industry who were wolves in sheep's clothing. I began to shrink away from a world that held significance for me. Could what Joe said be true? Did I know what I was talking about or was it just rhetoric? Family members said that I scared them, and my child said that I was a wild crazy woman.

Eventually, he did not want to hear any of my rhetoric and suggested I keep my beliefs to myself. If I did things with friends, a pattern of punishment would follow. Joe had love, I had seen it and felt it, but these were unhealthy qualities that raised flags. I found myself wanting to lie for fear of his reaction. I looked at him and I could see he loved me, and I could also see when he was in fear or feeling insecure. Our relationship began to feel turbulent for me.

We went on a holiday together which was amazing in many ways, but something happened that was a big warning for me. I began to feel very disempowered. We were walking along the rocks beside the ocean, and I thought, *Am I living Joe's will?*. I immediately fell, smashing my head on a rock, exactly the way you would see someone fall to their death in the movies. I lay there, stunned about what just happened. He called out to me. When I got up, I did not mention the thought I had at the moment when I fell. Later, he went to town, and I was to meet him. I was late because I did a mini yoga practice and did not message him to let him know. When I met up with him, he was very displeased and let me know my behavior was extremely disrespectful. We went into the store where he was going to buy me gloves for bike riding. I was not in the mood. I later asked him to not spend any money on me. I did not want him to buy me things. I appreciated his honesty and directness, but I also felt at times he was too harsh with me. Joe also said I should be more humble and that he felt I was full of ego.

I shared my feelings with my girlfriend, and she warned me that he sounded narcissistic, in ways he was gaslighting, and love bombing. He said he desired to die egoless. I felt that he had been in denial of his ego with his treatment towards me, which was a dangerous thing. We all have egos; the key is to recognize when we are in the ego state, which is part of who we are as human beings.

After we returned, Joe had little time for me. He was admittedly a work alcoholic He did a check-in each morning at 4:30 am and again in the evenings. Eventually, he admitted he did not want a relationship as it was too difficult to manage the commitment because the pressure of work was at its peak.

The energy between us remained undeniable, and even though he did not want a relationship, we played sexually online, and when he came to town, we spent time together. It seemed to me that he gave me as much time as he did to clean his toilets which was a job he loathed. I finally learned that work was his priority and a big responsibility. My pattern was to give all of myself to a relationship. He played with different rules, and it affected me on an emotional level. He told me to have patience, as winter would come and he would then again have time. It felt like a hot and cold relationship, and it was extremely confusing and painful. I constantly rode a rollercoaster of emotions. Yet, neither of us could let go.

The thing that kept me connected to him was the energy that was between us. I'd never felt anything like it before. We would be synchronistical in thinking of one another, taking pictures of sunsets, and sending them at the same time. When we were together, we had fun and shared plenty of exciting adventures. Being with Joe opened me up on a deeper level and I felt it. I realized it was Joe that I smashed to the ground when I fell on my walk, except, it was never about Joe. It was all about me and my growth in consciousness. Or was it a spiritual battle with fears and darkness holding me back? Joe wanted me to grow up and I admit I had some growing up to do. I started to recognize his patterns, and when he lied to me as a punishment, I immediately saw it and projected it back to him. I was becoming less triggered and noticed when he was projecting on me. I stopped taking it personally. One day I walked away from Joe after he lied, ending our relationship. The next day, he was in his car driving for five hours to see me. He had left a voicemail to inform me that he was on his way and that if I did not want to see him then I should not be available.

I instantly felt fear and wanted to run. I knew Joe would never physically hurt me; however, the instinct was sharp, forcing me to breathe deeply. It was my inner child who wanted to run, the one who was afraid she would lose the loving affection she'd found with Joe. I visualized her sitting on my lap and informed her that she was safe and that she was loved.

Joe arrived in town, and with courage, I faced him. I stood before him in the doorway, and he asked me to step closer to him. He hugged me and said let's be friends. I immediately felt free and went upstairs to my loft to sing and play music. Joe later admitted he felt jealous when he heard me singing, acknowledging to himself that he wanted me to be happy even if it was without him. Our relationship was far from being over.

I had a dream of my youngest child where I watched as she climbed to the top of a mountain and repeatedly threw herself off a cliff. I felt the dream represented my relationship with Joe and the cycle would only keep repeating itself. I waited patiently. When the spirit wanted me to move, I would know. I did not know how much more I could handle emotionally or mentally.

Love that Binds

I had returned to Grande Prairie several times to visit my girls. I missed having easy, quality time with them. Then an opportunity presented itself to return to the mansion where I had stayed on one of my visits. The attraction was to have more time with my family and the opportunity for a dream to come true to host yoga, horse, and leadership retreats. The mansion had a lot of rooms and the vision for a wellness center was an exciting opportunity for the ruler, maverick and celebrity archetypes in me. I spoke to the owner about my vision, and we agreed that while we did not know how it would unfold, we would be open and willing to figure it out along the way.

Driving back to Grande Prairie, I received a call from a very close friend, and I mentioned that I had some hesitation and felt uncertain about this partnership. She assured me that was normal. I also knew that even though I was moving into a *Grande* mansion, it was still a basement suite, which made me feel uncomfortable as I vowed to never live in one again.

I also needed to plan a trip to Newfoundland to see my mother who, at the age of sixty-five, was diagnosed with brain and lung cancer.

I could not fly previously because of the pandemic restrictions. Now I could go, and a girlfriend of mine, who happened to be the one I borrowed my wedding dress from for my first marriage, made the trip with me. She needed healing and time away for herself, having been in a deep grieving state since she lost her true love four years ago. She randomly happened to message me the very night I booked my flight. I had been waiting for years to hear from her and I said, "I just booked a flight, come with me," so she did.

Fresh ocean air and good people are food for the soul. She later admitted the trip saved her life and gave her the strength she needed to finally move forward. She too had been in an abusive relationship after the death of her husband and had been suffering in silence for too long. She was breaking her chains to be free. The most amazing thing after all of these years was the synchronicities that we had in common. When we first met, we were stay-at-home moms who ended up as divorcees and both worked successful careers in the financial industry. She watched me silently on social media for a long time before she reached out. She said the words I spoke were speaking to her soul. She revealed herself as a woman who was highly intuitive and experienced energy in amazing ways. She is very in tune with her cats and is known as the cat whisperer amongst her family members. I was glad she was going with me.

I did not know what to expect when I saw my mom. Luckily, I had a conversation with my aunt who warned me that mom had lost a lot of weight, and she hoped that I could extend some healing energy to her. Seeing her wasn't as bad as I had anticipated, which was a good thing.

My dad had died a year prior of a heart attack and I was not ready to lose my mom. I do believe our essence leaves our body and the energy continues into other lives. I have always believed that life is heaven or hell on earth as we choose to live it.

My younger brother picked me and my friend up from the airport. After dropping my friend off in my hometown of Port-Aux-Basques, we headed towards Codroy Valley, my favorite place next to my mountainous home in British Columbia.

I laid eyes on my mother and hugged her tight. I love you, Mom. I would spend the next twelve days spoiled by her home-cooked meals and campfires at night. Mom always loved to cook, and it gave her a sense of purpose to cook special foods from our new food culture. We had lovely evenings at the beach. Although I arranged a boat trip to the small town of Petites for us, Mom didn't feel strong enough to make the trip. I made the trip with friends instead, exploring the old, abandoned town. I playfully called for whales, but none were to be seen. Words did not come easily to me in conversations with my mom, but it really didn't matter. Our time together is what mattered. She started to eat a little more and her hair grew back by the end of our visit. My aunt was happy to see her sister looking a little brighter and so was I. Since I'd returned home, her cancer had not spread, even though it is labeled terminal. For the first time in our lives, my Christmas Mom acknowledged that she had always felt like the Grinch, but not this year. She was going to enjoy it. I was glad, that while she may not heal in the body I felt she was healing within her soul. My mother has spoken words that will forever be etched in my mind.

"Janet, I see what you are doing."

"Oh?"

"You are breaking the chains of our family."

"Yes, I guess I am."

"I am so proud of you," she said.

My mother is my biggest cheerleader. She has been there for me my entire life. Going through my divorce she helped, and I did not have to ask. She knew I needed it. And that was enough. When I first started to write publicly about my life, it was not easy for her. At first, I knew she felt shame. She admitted to me that she felt like a bad mother, placing me up for adoption and struggling with herself to express love. It did not feel good for her. I assured her that was part of the past, and that I held no resentment towards her. I loved her, always. Over time, I think hearing me talk about it helped set her free. Our lives were nothing to be ashamed of as all of us have shame and guilt that need healing. When we know better, we do better. Sometimes we know better and still do not do better. It is all part of our journey. I know she was feeling proud when she started to share a magazine article about me with others.

Love should never be a hard thing to express. Not being shown love as a young girl opened my heart desire to be both loving and affectionate with all my children. Each time my children and I speak with one another, we express words of love, and adoring compliments flow easily. I value the way we hug and kiss each other every time we see one another and again when we part. They always tried to figure out which of them I favor the most. My response was and is that I love them all equally. I could not ask to be blessed with more amazing children who are equally independent and strong. I am so proud and all my prayers for them continue to be answered.

My oldest is a teacher, a career that she was born to do. Her students and the entire school adore her. No one believes her age as she looks like a teenager. She is intelligent, with a big, beautiful smile. She is compassionate and kind to everyone around her.

The second in line is thriving in her own business and a homeowner at a young age. She is sensitive and intuitive. She openly communicates with me about everything in her life. She has some shyness about her, yet she is courageous and stands up for herself.

My youngest child is witty, wise, and brave.

All of them can ride a horse bareback through a field with only a halter. They spent the last three years working with horses which I know was healing and a dream come true for them. I admire my children deeply.

As I said, what more can a mom ask for? Quality time and touch are my love language. Vacations together, and sharing new experiences are what I desire for us. Returning to Grande Prairie was important for me and them. I felt that my healing journey over the years had been selfish, and I did things that created pain for them. For that, I am deeply sorry. I have apologized and asked for forgiveness. My middle child will often assure me, that although they experienced some tough challenges when their dad and I divorced, they too learned lessons that shaped them into becoming who they are today. I like to believe that I laid a strong foundation of love. Being a stay-at-home parent, I got to read to them at night and woke them in the morning with a pleasant, "Good morning, it's time to get up." I packed special love notes in their lunch bags. I was not perfect, and I had to learn to become a better mom. Being a parent does not come with a rule book. The very best gift I could give them was healing myself so we could enjoy our lives together bathed in so much love.

Love matters. Love is the solution. Love is the essence of who we are. This is the core of my beliefs.

Love Endings

My second husband and I didn't talk much during our separation period. I received my separation papers on Christmas Eve of 2021. He was the first to file. I was going to be the one to file the divorce documents, but he beat me to it. We spent twelve years together and I loved him with all my heart and soul. He was a kind and open man. We never shared spiritual beliefs and he would often joke he was a chicken-shit atheist.

In the end, it would be a separation of beliefs and resentment as he ran out of patience with all my changes and how we viewed money. Part of my drive to succeed was because I wanted to pay him back monetarily. I risked too much investing in my business. That was not in his comfort zone. I will be forever grateful for the love we shared. I wrote him a letter in the early part of our separation, and I do not know if he read it. He'd made up his mind that he was done with me. He ripped all parts of me out of our home immediately and spoke openly of his resentment about how I spent my money in a business he was not willing to understand or support. I did not ask for much when I left;

however, he may tell a different story. I sacrificed for him as well. That is not what I want to talk about here.

Returning to Grande Prairie meant I had to heal the wounds of my heart. He came to see me one day to deliver my mail. I felt guarded as he got out of his vehicle. At first, the questions were about family, our mothers, and kids. He was always a great stepdad to my youngest and will continue to be. I'm happy they have a close relationship.

He asked me if I was still doing my business.

"Yes."

"Are you doing anything else?"

"No."

"You know," he told me, "I am over all of the things about money."

"Okay."

"We could still be living our lives together."

Silence.

"But none of that matters now."

Silence.

We said our goodbyes. I walked into the mansion, sat at my computer, and cried. What did he mean, *we could still be together?* If what? If I had not changed careers or invested in a business. Or he had not avoided his emotions and was willing to communicate his feelings or try to go a little deeper for the sake of our relationship.

I texted to ask him what he meant, adding he did not have to reply. He never did. It doesn't matter, it's over. It was a dream come true for a while. He did leave me with an amazing gift, Leo my cocker spaniel, the best Christmas present a girl could have received. That dog is my companion and brings me tremendous joy.

I cried randomly after that for a couple of weeks. I would even text him, asking if he would be willing to have a conversation sometime. He wanted to think about it and said he would get back to me. He messaged several hours later, to say, "As long as I have to pay you alimony, I have nothing to say to you to help you in your healing journey."

That was okay with me, as immediately after I had asked, I made peace with my story, so I did not need to discuss it with him. What mattered was what I knew to be true for me.

Shortly after that exchange, we crossed paths at the grocery store. What were the chances that both of us would be in the same place at the same time, meeting in the center of the aisle?

"Good morning," I was the first to speak.

"Fancy meeting you here."

"Yes," he grinned. "Timing."

I said, "I am making chili and looking for kidney beans."

He said, "I'm looking for black beans." Probably making one of his famous casseroles.

I walked into the next aisle, and he called out to me. "Janet, they are over here."

I thanked him. He was unaware that we walked out together. He was at the cashier, directly in front of me. We both paid and I followed behind him. He stopped at Starbucks just ahead of me, I called out to him, "Have a good day!"

Surprised, he said, "You too."

I felt completely free. I believed this was divine timing and a message for me that we were complete, and that my heart had healed a little more.

Which brings me back to Joe. When I returned from Newfoundland, I landed at the airport in Edmonton. I'd planted the seed with Joe that I was only eight hours away and would love to see him. I needed to see him. I needed to be held by him. However, he stated that he was busy and that I could not visit. I was in turmoil. I parked my truck on the highway and had a huge temper tantrum. I felt like the little girl in the book *Think and Grow Rich*, which I have read at least ten times. It was a story of persistence where the little girl had been sent by her mother to retrieve fifty cents from the neighbor. She did not back down from the full-grown man who insisted that she go away. She stood firm, even when he charged towards her. In the end, he gave her what she wanted. Joe knew I was having a meltdown and softened, agreeing to let me visit. My happiness mattered to him; he just had a difficult time prioritizing it at times.

Joe later mentioned he failed to realize that I only needed to be loved and held after seeing my mother. We had a lovely weekend together, time in the mountains where we fished, and he assisted me in catching my first trout together. We swam in the river and enjoyed quality time.

My move to Grande Prairie hurt Joe. It was difficult putting a boundary between us.

Earlier in the year I had sent an application to speak at the Kootenay Yoga festival after receiving an intuitive sensation to apply. I would be right there in the area where Joe was. I was so excited to go. At that moment, I did not have the money, and when I told Joe, he advised against it, saying it wasn't a wise business move. However, that week I signed up new clients and had the money to go. Joe still said I could not visit him. I could not understand. Then he said he was seeing someone else. It hurt. It felt as if he were punishing me for moving or for attending the yoga retreat. I arrived in the little mountainous town and spent the night at a dear friend's home. The next morning, Joe and I had a brief time together on the phone where I cried. I told him, that loving him was hurting me.

That day, I drove to the yoga festival. My heart and head hurt. I walked around to explore where I would be teaching the next morning. I attended one yoga class and left. My energy was extremely heavy, and I was hurting. I booked myself a room in an Airbnb. I called my best soul sister, and I talked about how I was feeling. She listened as I questioned my sanity and this relationship. I blocked Joe once again. I had to let go. It was too much, and I was risking my mental and emotional well-being.

My friend assured me, "You and only you are responsible. You keep letting him in."

I went to bed early that night. It was important for me to be rested to teach the next day. I came all this way, and it was important to me.

The next morning, I woke with a deep sense of my inner child and felt my father's presence. It was my inner child that wanted Joe so badly. He was the only man who gave me love, affection, and attention in that way. It was my inner child who longed for the love she missed receiving from her father. I visualized sitting her on my lap and putting my arms around her and told her, once again, how much she was loved, and that she did not deserve the pain she experienced growing up. I told her she was safe and secure. That she is deserving and worthy of so much more. My father whispered in my ear that I deserved love and not the kind he provided for me and not the kind of love that Joe was giving me. It wasn't real love. It was love tangled with control, manipulations, and lies. This was the kind of love that I needed to release.

It was at that very moment that I had a deep realization about the work I was doing and the tools I was providing to support mental and emotional wellness. My father suffered because he did not have the tools to navigate through his own life's challenges, and it was the same for my mother. Life's experiences can be hard, pain is often inevitable, and yet pain is required for our growth. That said, with proper tools and strategies it does not have to be so hard. More importantly, with a deeper connection to God, our pain is lessened as we can experience his grace through receiving spirit. My work is the legacy of my father and my mother. It was a profound moment for me.

I was ready to begin my day, I drove an hour just outside Nelson to speak at the yoga festival. Before I would teach my session with twenty men and women, I got to experience transcendental dance for the first time. It was amazing. My body moved freely and wildly. I loved every single second of the dance, the deep connection to breathing, releasing, and letting go was powerful. Freeing. It was for me, at that moment, divine. I delivered a conversation to open-hearted Yogis who were ready to receive. For an hour, I talked about energy bodies, archetypes, and our relationship to money and what it can teach us. The conversations were brilliant. The participants opened up to discuss their feelings of resistance, excitement, heaviness, and curiosity about emotions surrounding money. We concluded that facing those emotions was the pathway to higher consciousness. I received hugs, mostly from the men in the room.

Later, I would sign up and work with my first couple. It was an honor for me. And it was profound for them. I was meant to be there that weekend for so many reasons. My soul let me know by the excitement I felt when I first applied. I knew, beyond a doubt, that I was supposed to be there. It was perfectly and divinely orchestrated.

I'd like to close this part of the book with an *OM*. A powerful mantra chanted in yoga designed for manifesting positive things in life. Breathe in…..now out…….OM

I returned to Grande Prairie. Joe remained in my heart and mind. We blocked each other's communications, only to unblock so we could send or receive a message. A part of me still wanted to share my life with him. Each time I opened the pathway, I felt fear in my heart. Three weeks went by. I moved out of the mansion and into my new place. I unconsciously unblocked him and received his text.

Did I let him in? Of course, I let him in. We decided to take a trip to Bragg Creek to spend a weekend together. I thought this weekend would tell if we continued or if would we end our on-and-off-again relationship. He shared that he had the same thought. Once again, our weekend together was filled with conversation and adventures. We walked along a riverbank where Joe encouraged me to climb up the side. It was steep, and it felt like the side of a mountain. We had to climb up to get around. I started to climb. I was afraid and panicked. I did not like it. I was afraid of falling. Joe talked me through it, and it was not easy. I'd had a similar experience with him in Sooke on Vancouver Island. Joe had a way of guiding me through fear both internally and physically. Yet Joe would cause more fear to rise in me than anyone I have ever met. Fear was rising because I was losing connection with what was important to me. I was allowing Joe to have superiority over me. Why was I not standing in power?

I returned home, and I resisted telling him about a speaking event I had the very next weekend in Red Deer at a women's conference. I knew he did not like the celebrity archetype in me who wanted to be out there creating an impact and recognition.

So, on the very day I got in my car to drive to Red Deer, I confessed.

He said, "You waited until now to tell me?"

"Yes."

He did not say anything. But I knew that he would process what I said, and I would receive some punishment later.

My speech was like the one I presented on stage at Blu Talks in Edmonton the day before I left for Newfoundland to see my mom. It was still very new and when I spoke, I had to pause to check my notes. Anytime I speak, I give myself full permission to simply do it knowing that I am enough, and I will do my best in the moment. That was Louise Hay's advice, speak your best from a place of being enough and then later, ask yourself what you could have done differently. There were about fifty women in the room, and I was the first speaker of the day. My money talk was vulnerable, and it opened the door for other women to speak up. Money can bring about plenty of resistance. A woman spoke up to ask, as a stay-at-home mom who was not earning money, how can she own her worth?

I asked her and the audience to turn their attention towards themselves to discover their worth:

"If I were to ask you to sell me your eyes for a million dollars, would you?"

"No," she replied.

"How about your heart, your brain, and your organs?"

"No," she replied.

"Now take a moment to inventory your assets, including your gifts and other talents. What do you think the price would be?"

"Priceless" she replied.

"Now, I added, "let's look at your liabilities, your fears, your indebtedness to others, your secrets, and feelings of guilt or shame. What do those liabilities cost you?

She paused. "This will take some work."

What happens when you blame, criticize, or judge? Are you living in love or fear in those moments? When you behave in those behaviors or speak words that detract from your value and worth, pause for a moment, and let that sink in. If you viewed yourself as being sacred, how would you treat yourself?

You are already worthy. You just need healthier boundaries.

You are blind to enlightened net worth and need more understanding of yourself.

Do your liabilities rob you of being connected to the highest essence of yourself? *You are always divided within yourself in the moments you are not connected to your truth, which is love.*

I talked about how, unfortunately, more value is placed on the man as the provider and not the woman who often is the nurturer and supporter. In reality, we both play an important role and are equally valuable. And yet we fail one another, measuring our value and having the one who makes the most money have of greater worth. This is a liability to many relationships. We view others as having greater importance because of the amount of money they make. We even put our happiness in money, saying things like I will be happy when I have more money. We know this is not true, however, it has been a pattern that has been repeating for far too long and it is damaging to humans living in this world at these times. What if the currency of money changes, and instead we give value to one another by being in service to one another in more helpful, compassionate ways that are not dominated by money?

When I have asked this question before, women will sometimes confess that they find it difficult to put a price tag on themselves, yet if you ask to see another's worth or if they see it in their children then the answer to define worth is easy. It is easy to see the worth of another and yet we fail to see our own. This is why relationships are so important for our growth. It is in relationships that we see ourselves. We spend our lives building our net worth, but we are disconnected from our enlightened net worth. Instead, let us ask, trust, and have the patience to receive what is given to us from the universe, from God.

When I concluded, there was silence in the room. The day was a win. I was acknowledged by one of my fellow speakers as having a calm energy and that she had looked forward to meeting me in person to experience it. It was a nice compliment.

I left the event to spend the night at a girlfriend's house where I would connect with her oldest daughter. This family is still healing from the loss of a man they deeply loved. The daughter told me after my last visit, strange things started to happen to her, and she wanted to understand more about energy. We talked and I shared what I knew to answer her curiosity. I told her to reach out to me anytime, and that I would be there as a guide to support her when needed. In her twenties, she experienced plenty of challenges with boys, drugs, and self-esteem. Her wisdom and curiosity at such a young age were a delight to see and reminded me of myself. When the conversation started to get heavy, I encouraged us to dance to move the heavy energy that was encompassing the room.

In the meantime, I received non-stop text messages from Joe, which was exactly what I expected. He was going to beat me up. I don't recall his words, but they were punitive. I was deceitful and to him, that meant I was living in fear. I tried to explain that I did not, that I knew I would tell him, but I held back because I knew he would not approve of my speaking at an event. He did not trust me being in a room filled with people, my guess is mostly men. His lack of trust was within himself, and he projected that onto me.

He commented, "Your perception of deceit is different from the rest of the world."

I felt he did not create an environment in which I felt safe. Even if Joe was right and I was living in fear, I did not need his approval to do something important to me. This time, what he had to say to me, had no impact. I was completely detached from his punishment. I knew after I left the yoga festival that I would never allow a man to mentally and emotionally impact me that way again. I was free from this pattern of verbal abuse. I was solid in myself, and I did not need his approval or punishment. There was no emotional triggering within me.

I returned home the next day. I thought this time we were done. Until I heard from Joe the following day. He messaged me about the weather. I asked, why are you messaging me? Do you want to talk about the weather, or do you miss me?

I had changed. There was no longer a need for a man within me. That week, I prepared myself for another talk. This one was in the place where I lived for the past 15 years, and there was a little fear in me around the opinions of others. I breathed deeply to let this awareness of fear go. I wanted to adjust and strengthen my speech, so I reached out to a speaking expert I met on LinkedIn, sending my existing speech and asking him for help.

He said some things that made me pay attention. "You are like a Ferrari moving forward fast, yet you are like a station wagon with a trunk full of stuff."

I took in his words. I needed to hear them and process them. I told him I had to deliver my talk the next day and I did not need a deep dive, just help to reshape it so I could be more effective in connecting with the audience. While I liked my previous two speeches, I had spoken to more than one hundred people, and no one reached out to me for work. Something was not right. He gave me strategies to "Captivate, Educate, and Motivate" my audience. I went to bed that night recreating my talk to fit those strategies. It would be different from my first two as the focus was more on my story, our energy bodies, and the power of archetypes and money. I had been hot-flashing like crazy for weeks and had not been sleeping well. Still, I showed up confidently at the networking leadership event held by the Mental Wellness Matters Society. There were two female speakers and one male as the MC. I was going to read my notes and get grounded, but instead talked with a female entrepreneur I knew. She asked me about my marriage and what had happened. Her impression was that I had been living my dream life. I advised her I was, but the universe had much more for me to experience. The conversation was a distraction. I felt I might forget everything I had to say as my mind kept going blank. I sat and listened to the first speaker, who was setting the stage perfectly for my talk with her words. It was my turn. I took a deep breath, looked up to God, and said *you are up*! I calmly delivered the most relaxed speech. I engaged the audience with questions, and it flowed divinely. When it was all over, the comment was that I was born to be on stage and people were curious to know more about energy, archetypes, and our relationship with money.

Instead of basking in the positive feedback and responses, I felt defeated. My bank account had a negative balance for the second time. I felt I had done my absolute best, and yet, I did not receive any new clients over the fall. I honestly felt I was done. I did not need to talk, write, or give myself to anyone or anything. I retreated into the holidays. It was time to remove the junk from my trunk.

Letting Go

The journey to author this book first began in 2018 when I asked a woman I met through my insurance business if she would be a ghostwriter for my book. I knew I had a story to tell, and I just did not know how to tell it. I thought, *what am I doing asking a woman from Zimbabwe to author my story?* Her thought was similar: *what is this white woman from Newfoundland doing, asking me to write her story?* Still, she said yes, and we began our journey together. I felt we were divinely connected to do this. I paid her six thousand dollars up front and handed her a compilation of my writings. We met on a couple of occasions, and she asked me questions. I trusted the process and gave it over to her. Then I did not hear from her for a long time. It was not until after I moved to the little mountain town in BC that we came together to complete the process. I paid her flight down and cleared my schedule for the week so we could have time together. We walked and talked. She wanted to get a better understanding of me. She admitted that she did not like me. She felt I spoke too much and that my experiences had a lot of darkness. She spent time in prayer to try to understand me. On one of our walks, she spoke about her mother.

Then I saw it, and asked, "Do I remind you of your mother?" Yes, she confessed, very much. You helped me to heal my relationship with my mother." Her mother was in search of personal development and at times it impacted her family negatively. I could understand how she would have felt critical about my actions, and I understood the similar impact they had on my own family. We sat in the local library where she shared with me for the first time the words she had written about me in my book, which would be titled *Cracked Open. A journey of looking at the uncomfortable parts of self, to live a life of consciousness.*

I wept as I read those words in the corner of the library that day, and my heart opened. I could see the vulnerability as an opening for others to crack open and heal. It was good, it was really good.

We both felt it might have a big impact on other readers who would be seeking similar desires as mine. We were excited and thrilled about the possibilities of what this book might bring into the world. When she first arrived, she asked me a question.

"Are you sure you want to bring this book into the world? People could crucify you."

I said, "This book is no longer about me. It is about sharing my story to help others who need healing in this world. It will be written."

After reading her draft, I saw that there was no mention of my first husband. I asked her why, as he played an important role in my growth. She noted that from our earlier conversations, I seemed upset when we first began discussing his role. You see, I had not yet forgiven him for what he did to our children. Of course, he was not the only person responsible for our children's wounds. I have since found deeper understanding and forgiveness around the pain we both inflicted.

She felt he was in the eye of the storm, so we went for a walk in the woods, and I tried to give her a better understanding of our relationship together. At the end of our talk, we stood still in the silence of the woods.

She backed away from me and said, "Everyone in your life has been a casualty of yours. Your first and second husband, your children. Others as well."

I received her words, and they washed over me with a heavy sensation. I felt like I wanted to end my life. I paused and replied, "And yet, here I am."

She returned to Grande Prairie, and it was not until a visit in March that she first informed me that she was done with the book.

I was shocked, "You are done. Why didn't you tell me?"

I would never see that draft of my manuscript, as the following week, her computer crashed, and she had no backup. I bought her a new laptop and she agreed to begin again in a series of three parts. I had hired a publishing company and had already made the payments; the cover had also been designed. The dates were set, and the book would be ready for publication on November 9th, my mother's birthday. The first chapter had been completed, I eagerly sent it out to friends for review without reading it myself. When I did read it, two parts did not feel right to me. It was not from my perspective. I emailed to ask her to make the change and I offended her. She texted me, "I am not your punching bag, I am just your writer."

"Whoa, wait a minute," I told her. "I would never want you to feel like that. You are more than my writer. If you feel that way, I am so sorry, as that is not my intention at all."

I shared some of the reviews from my friends. Some said they loved it, while others could tell her writing apart from my story. I emailed her to say, take time, look into your own heart to ask if you want to complete this journey. It is okay to say no to me. She replied that she would finish it and would meet the deadline, but she was leaving for a trip. The deadline came and went, and I heard nothing.

Fourteen days past the deadline, we met over a Zoom call. I could sense the energy before she arrived. It did not feel good. I asked, "How are you? Is everything okay?"

"Yes," she answered.

"What about the book?" I asked.

"Before we talk about that," she said, "I have something to say to you. You are a manipulative woman. You are on a high horse."

"Perfect," I said. I needed to know where we were, and I just received my answer.

She was furious. "I do not like you. I am getting off this call." That would be the last time we talked except through the lawyer as I requested a partial refund for the book not being completed. In those follow-up legal conversations, she said I was not being honest, portraying myself as a prosperous woman with my background of poverty, drugs, and promiscuity.

Her words hurt me deeply. Truth is malleable. Her perceptions were different from mine. I understood that. There was no point in fighting.

I needed to let go. So, I did. I dropped any legal proceedings. It would be a waste of time, energy, and money.

I reached out to ask Joe if I could spend a couple of days at the lake house, and along with her chapter and my writings, I put together the book. I asked my editor friend who had written an article about me in the Synergy magazine to complete the editing. Over the Christmas holidays, as I began to let go and forgive, I began to get a sense that I needed to let go of that book entirely, as the experience I had with my ghostwriter made it all feel dirty. That is when I knew I would begin writing this book, with the title that had appeared in my previous dream *Heal Your Money, Heal Your Life.*

I spoke with my past editor, who had also become a trusted and dear friend. She confirmed what I had sensed, that while the book was a combination of an autobiography, self-help, and inspiration, it was something else. And it was not finished. I thanked her for her openness and honesty. I valued that in a friendship. I surrendered that book once and for all and let go.

On January 4th, I woke up with a sense of urgency to write. I set the intention to let spirit guide me in writing a new book, this book. I committed to writing by clearing space for creative flow and completed this book in five days, two days before my dad's birthday on January 8th. On January 9th, I would begin a new career at RBC, accepting an offer once again. It was the thought of being in a nine-to-five career again that propelled me to get my story down, this time it was from a different place within myself. This is the question I asked:

If you are to be the star of your financial future three years from now, what habits would you transform today?

The experience with my writer revealed habits and patterns that I needed to let go of. The pattern I recognized was handing off my responsibility to someone else. I did pay her to do a job, but I failed to have boundaries. I trusted her more than I trusted myself and my ability to write my own story. I am grateful for the experience, yet it has been a common theme for me to rely on someone else in my life because of a deep-rooted belief that I am not enough on my own. When I was first married, I did not feel capable of being a single parent, so I remained in an unhealthy marriage. Even in financial matters, I had relied on a man my whole life for something I only strived for yet failed to achieve. I did achieve it while working at the bank. In my personal work – my passionate work – I felt insecure. This insecurity kept me in unhealthy relationships. I had some growing up to do. Sure, I had help from others uncovering my story. All my relationships were a mirror and a guide for me to see my inner brilliance or the higher parts that existed within me, but I focused too much on not being enough.

No one can write our story for us. No one is capable of knowing the real person inside of us. It is for each of us to discover. Also, we need each other to grow and to see ourselves. When we understand fully the power we have access to, we begin to use it differently. We look within more than to the outside world.

Looking back at my money relationships, I gave and spent carelessly and impulsively, as if I had to prove something. I was driven from a place inside myself that was not spiritual. I finally saw that I was driven by desires and the pursuit of money. This was not what God wanted of me. I was serving two masters until the day I realized this and made a choice to get clear about whom I was serving.

Whom Was I Serving?

"If a house is divided against itself, that house cannot stand."

MARK 3:25

I needed to learn to stand in my power, independent of a man. I appreciate the words of this verse, as I feel divided as long as I am serving from a place of fear. My intuition is guiding me toward achieving my highest self through my thoughts, emotions, and actions. When I am out of alignment, I will fall and keep falling until I learn the lesson.

I prayed to God to help me expand his territory, to let me serve his will, not mine. I asked that he protect me from evil. In reality, I served my own will, therefore many of my plans were met with frustration and failures.

All experiences are filtered through the lens of our story, our motivations, and our fears. The key is to know ourselves and open our hearts by freeing them from our ego trickery, so we can feel God's presence and learn what he wants to create through us. We get there through emotional mastery and knowing ourselves. When I am in a place of alignment, which for me means being in integrity and connected to God, it is because I've spent time connecting to him.

In the morning or throughout the day, I feel the energy of emotions in my body. If it is right, it feels peaceful. If it is wrong, I feel a heavy drain on my energy. Being more in tune with my spirit and being open and in alignment helps guide me on my path in life. Most of the world is not connected in this way. I realize the importance of identifying to whom and what I give my attention, as well as the need to protect myself with healthier boundaries. Allowing people or possessions to have power over us often creates repetitious chaos and confusion. We keep indulging in self-sabotaging patterns and behaviors trapped in a cycle from which our soul longs to break free. I am learning to ask for protection from God when I think negatively or hear the judgments of my mind at the time they occur, and it works. In those moments when I ask, I receive support and the protection I need.

"From what source am I creating?" This is a powerful question. Is it from my wounds created by a hurtful experience? Am I blocking opportunities and the possibility of achieving more love and experiencing more from life on my terms because of my judgments and limited thinking? Am I returning to an old pattern versus rising above to achieve my highest levels?

I have learned that when I create from the space of fear, I contract; and by contrast, creating from a place of love, I expand and flow. In the Bible, it is written that God is our creator, and that pain is used to shape our hearts…that God is love and we are loved dearly by him, that in fact, I am an expression of love made by him. Becoming a teacher is the expression of spirit moving through me that I cherish and hold as a reverent place. It is a place I wish to be in more of the time. For me, it is living in heaven on earth versus the struggle of living in hell on earth. It connects me to the love of God, and I extend that love to myself. It takes a serious commitment to get here and stay here. I lived in a high place of love for a period, thinking I could not lose it. I was wrong. I can and have lost it and many times. I must return each time to cleanse my house of the patterns and fears that I'd had in the past.

Not surrendering the past, is not fully living in the present.

Stay with me as my story reveals my discovery of more truth. I've been completely stripped down, lost myself only to go deeper, surrendered my life entirely to God and his will, and let go of my own will to find my greatest self again. I feel grateful to be a visionary as my dreams and the guidance I receive reveals the greater picture.

I read a post on LinkedIn from Danny Langloss, a well-known keynote speaker, Dixon City Manager, and retired police chief. I connected with him through an ecosystem of like-minded individuals whose common goal is to create positive change in this world. His message was about psychological safety versus contributory dissent, and in his message, he quoted Amy Edmondson, of The Harvard Business School, who writes:

> *"Leaders are looking to create psychological safety in the workplace, which includes the belief that one will not be punished or humiliated*

for speaking up with ideas, questions, concerns, or mistakes, and when psychological safety is high, creativity, innovation, ownership, and wellness thrive. Contributory dissent is the expectation that everyone will contribute to the discussion, solve a problem, or speak up when they see an issue or a problem. This includes the best-effort ideas, speaking firmly and frankly, and sharing without malice or negative connotation. The one thing that resonated for me the most is once a leader demonstrates contributory dissent, the leader will own the decision made by the top leader as their idea. This is referred to as one-voice leadership. One-voiced leadership is one of the most important factors in creating winning cultures and championship teams because a house divided cannot stand on its own (Langloss)."

Who is this one-voice leader? Can they hold empathy, compassion, kindness, and love within our environment? Aren't we all leaders in our lives creating a safe space within ourselves, our family, and in our community. Are we safe people? Can someone speak firmly and frankly without our reacting from a fearful place? Can we disagree and still hold space of grace for one another? Within ourselves, we are divided by love or fear.

Can you feel an inner conflict within yourself? Imagine as an individual leader, feeling safe and capable enough to speak up without the insecurity and the fears that separate us within ourselves and from each other. We can expand internally by identifying the deep-seated beliefs and parts of our personality which we have hidden. Without awareness, our efforts to be in control of events in our lives will fail. What if, as leaders, we are no longer divided by fear but solid in our house of love connected to God as the creator in our lives?

Joe told me over and over to "Live life, Janet. It's a gift and not to be wasted." He also said, "If someone doesn't add to your life, get rid of them, cut the head off the beast, and don't try to save them." It is not my job to save someone, it is my job to save myself. It is my purpose to heal myself and inspire healing in others. He also reminded me to create the life I want without relying on others to provide it for me. I am guilty of staying in a relationship because I was living in fear. It took years for me to gain the courage to get out of my first marriage. And if I had listened to my soul in my second marriage, then perhaps so many others would not have suffered. I cannot change my past; however, I can learn from it as many times as it takes. I know I can decide my future by consciously choosing my words and thoughts and the relationships I choose to engage in. Words have power, and when we speak, they can lift us up or tear us down, including the words that we express inside ourselves. For years when I taught yoga, I would say these words to my students, "be gentle, be gentle, be gentle." When I stopped punishing myself internally, I crossed the line and was able to love myself more than I had previously because I'd stopped the pattern. The less I punished myself, the more loving I became. The more loving I became, the more I deepened my relationship with God. The more I saw his hand at work in my life. Trusting in myself and him became inevitable.

Letting go of the expectations of others is important, but most of all, I had to let go of the expectations I held of myself. Returning to

Grande Prairie, I realized that my marriage didn't just end because of money. It ended because I no longer fit the expectations of my husband. I didn't meet the expectations of my friend in the little mountainous town when we parted ways, or the expectations Joe placed upon me. My close friend said it best: "If you place expectations upon me, expect to be disappointed." Repeatedly, I would set high goals for myself, and over and over I would be disappointed. When I let go of expectations, I allowed myself to be guided more and with greater ease instead of striving because I had something to prove or because I wanted to be right about something. I am not saying that expectations are a bad thing. When in balance, they can be good. When out of balance, they can be harmful to our mental-emotional well-being. Expectations harmed my finances, as I always expected success to come faster than it would. I was compulsive in my spending, often valuing status above financial security. I could have allowed myself the opportunity to balance the risk with financial security by accepting the bank position and growing my business; however, that was not my choice at that time. This led to greater risk and the fall of my financial foundation. That said, I re-created my solid foundation using my tools and allowing myself to be completely guided. Everything always works out for me. I know this for certain.

When Joe looked at me, all he could see was my ego and his belief that I needed to become humbler. This was a fine line to walk because feeling high on love, joy, and specialness can push you into feeling superior. I did not view myself this way; however, when I visited my home on the island, I got a lesson in becoming humbler. In a conversation with an old friend, she shared how she struggled with her young daughter's illness, and she couldn't understand why it was happening to their family. I shared some of my thoughts. She said, "I don't know what you mean." I spent the night at her place and in the morning, sitting by the lake I asked God to help me find the words to explain. Later, she and I talked more, and she still didn't quite understand me. What I was trying to say is do not live in fear; learn to live in love. Fear would not extend her young daughter's life, but living in love might. I thought this. I did not say it.

It has taken me a while to recognize there is a difference in how I think. A close friend reminded me, "We are all and nothing at the same time." What would life look like if we could hold space for our differences and see the value in each other, as well as ourselves?

Let me expand on that thought: What does it mean to hold space with love, compassion, and kindness, rather than judgment, criticism, hate, or blame? So many times in my past, I ran from and repressed uncomfortable situations or conversations. When I was able to face them, I expanded my ability to embrace more of the qualities written above. My instinct to run was fear-based, survival-based. Now, in those moments I feel fear and there is no actual danger, I can be still and use the practice of pausing, holding space with my energy.

It is in the face of fear or chaos that we need to get grounded. We need to look around, notice how we are feeling on the inside, and look outside ourselves to determine if we are, in fact in danger or safe. Most times, we do not need to run. We can face the challenge and benefit from the growth and rewards that will follow. We give ourselves a chance by acknowledging "I am currently safe; however, my body requires rewiring after so many years of not being safe." Because I did not grow up in safety, I chose relationships with men who did not provide that element of safety. As the relationships evolved, if I stood up for myself or expressed my feelings, they felt threatened because they also didn't have the tools to navigate their emotions and deal with conflict.

Years ago I asked myself this question: "If I were to be the star of my financial future three years from now, what habits would I transform today?" I received this message: "Stop drinking alcohol." At the time, I was questioning if I had a drinking problem. The thought had consumed plenty of airspace in my mind. As soon I got the message, I called a friend in AA to say I had a problem and needed help. I attended AA for three months. Then I was on my own and did not drink for another fifteen months. Before asking for help, I was having trouble quitting on my own. Letting go of alcohol was what I needed to do at the time because it was part of a habitual pattern of boredom. Evenings at home were often spent in front of the television watching the same shows. Letting go of alcohol broke boredom and my habit, allowing me the space I needed to see the other things about my life that I needed to let go of. Wayne Dywer spoke about this in his book *Power of Intention*, by acknowledging that doing spiritual work requires sobriety. Here are a few things I've learned:

I can only control my actions by taking responsibility to be better as a human. I can allow myself to make mistakes. I can practice more empathy and it is easier when another person does the same. When someone is in blame or judgment, I have no issue walking away because they are not ready or willing to listen. In conversation with others, I show up, authentically myself. I speak up and enjoy soulful conversations. I enjoy conversations better when I can listen and be understood; to me, those are the best exchanges for growing a healthy relationship. I practice being kind, compassionate, and loving to everyone. I love to experience life and see the beauty in it. When someone is rude or projecting about who or what they think I am, I can sit in silence. When someone is rigid in their boundaries, it is because in the past they may have had a bad experience, and to prevent that bad experience from happening they have a rigid boundary. This can block the heart. Sometimes this is appropriate and other times it can create difficulties. People like this don't want to hear what you have to say. They are fixed in their opinions and judgments. When I experience this with others, I know they are blocking their opportunity to receive or give more love. It is like they built a wall to protect their hearts from being hurt once again. In such situations, I don't say anything. It is not my job to heal the world or change someone else. It is my job to heal myself so that I can know who I am. My job entails working with others who are open and willing to change by accepting the responsibility to do the work to heal. To do this I have to be willing to look inward, rather than blame or criticize others. Being responsible for myself means not giving away my power. With practice, awareness, and the right support in place, it will be done. I consider myself to be a vessel for spirit to work through and it's my job to clear myself so that I am open to receive and let the full expression of spirit move through me.

Here's my advice: Let go of the fear of losing. It can be hard to lose in relationships, life, or business. When my husband and I separated, I placed a card on his pillow before I left the house. It read *love is the solution*. I wanted him to move through his fears to find love. The truth is he reached the limits within himself; however, I know the capacity of love can hold so much space. We also didn't share the same beliefs which led to a division. Before the success of my spiritually-based business, our differences in beliefs were never an issue. When we parted ways, I used to sing out loud, *"Let love win."* The real truth was I needed to let love win within myself.

I can stand in my power rather than shrink in the presence of another person who holds their power. Fear had taken over my life and would remain there until the day I looked to God to bring me home. I consciously made choices to let go of important parts of myself and it was difficult; however, I discovered so much more because even in that place of fear, I welcomed the lessons it gave me. I would have to choose to walk the path to receive the love that I had been born with and had lost through my life experiences. No one could walk it for me, it would be my will to choose to make aligned choices that led me to my highest self. I did find the highest expression of myself, and I can say, it is heaven on earth. It is the space where everything flows. The most prosperous experiences for me are feeling love, joy, and harmony because I am connected to spirit. I am grateful for my devotion to seeking what was calling me.

Home is a welcoming loving place.

Love is always present.

What feels right for one person may not feel good for another.

The thing I realize is that I have always loved, regardless of what was done to me. I just had to learn to love myself more by looking at my fears and setting healthy boundaries, speaking up for myself, always standing up for what I feel is right, and letting go of what does not feel right. This is an act of love. Choosing ourselves is an expression of love even though it might be difficult for another to accept. I have not always listened to myself and have, at times, ignored myself. However, that voice inside is relentless and it has built a resiliency within me. I had to not be afraid to lose in relationships. I had to become more afraid of losing myself or my connection to God. The thing is, everyone wants to love and to be loved but most lack the tools or support to understand the role our fears play in robbing our lives of love.

Plato says true friendship can only exist between equals. This means to be in harmony we must have similar interests, move in the same direction, and be open to hearing and understanding one another. It is okay to disagree and have healthy conflict, as long as there is still safety. Is someone being harmed or devalued?

Friendships are integral for most people. My closest friends are of like mind and want to be and do better because we understand that who we are matters. We enjoy deep, open, soulful conversations where we can say absolutely anything to one another. We don't judge, condemn, or criticize. We are kind and honest. We seek to listen and understand or have a willingness to do so even if we fail. Throughout my life and relationships, I had to undo what love was not. I repeated the difficult lessons on many occasions. I set my boundaries from within and do not just accept what someone's opinion is regarding my life. I am free to choose and trust my own guidance. Healthy boundaries are liberating.

When my accounts went in the negative, it was challenging. I questioned how this could have happened. This is what I teach. I'd done the work. In this case, the universe used money to get my attention and redirect my actions. I wanted nothing more than to wave a wand and make my business a growing success, but God had something else in mind. How else could he get me to listen? I can be stubborn at times. Plus, it had been the pursuit of money that provided the opportunity to understand my enlightened self. What I needed was the embodiment of my enlightened net worth. I needed to see my value and worth and be willing to put the boundaries in place that showed my commitment to it, so I could heal on a deeper level. My pursuit of money was to build my net worth. To climb higher I needed to look at my beliefs and face my fears. This act freed me from my internal limits and helped me understand what my enlightened net worth meant. Who I am as love and light is beyond any material possessions.

It was time for me to get a job. At first, I avoided the bank. I had an interview with Canadian Mental Health Association and the interview was promising. When my friend asked how I felt about it, I said I didn't feel anything. I mentioned how my best option would be to apply to the bank; however, I felt I would have to eat a lot of humble pie. I declined three offers the previous year. They saw more value in me than I did in myself at the time. Why did I feel I needed to eat humble pie?

Something in me needed to be cleared. The next day, there was a posting. Coincidence? I applied and immediately sent an email to the branch manager. A rush of energy moved from my root chakra upward. It was freeing and exciting. Was I meant to do this? The following Tuesday, I had an interview. They told me things had changed since I'd worked there last. They added a big focus on emotional health for employees, and I immediately thought this was a good fit. I accepted the offer the next day, planning to begin in the new year.

My sense of energy was a result of me taking responsibility for my life. The thing is, I can plan in life, and yet God has a plan for me which can feel confusing at times. It requires patience and an even deeper need to remain grounded. If I am in fear of losing or am attached to expectations of how I want things to work, it can impede the process and block the flow. Knowing that I was going to walk into the new year with a guaranteed income of over eighty thousand settled my nervous system down and relaxed my body. My business had supported me with enough income over the past three years; however, I invested over sixty thousand, and having a salary provided me an income to meet my needs and my desire to continue growing my business. I immediately started to sleep better, and my hot flashes became non-existent.

I thought I had been moving through my challenges, and that I was ready for consistency and stability. I continued to believe that behind every challenge is a negative belief that doesn't serve me. The one that I uncovered throughout this process was that I can have both my needs and my desires met. My mother used to say, *you can have what you need but not what you want*. I was ready to let that belief go.

I had to let go of the lack to embrace the abundance that was within me. Being in fear prevented me from being in the flow of God. I had to let go of all of this to allow myself to feel inspired (in spirit). I began to feel in alignment again which opened the pathways to creativity and writing this book. Fear still showed up, but I welcomed it. I invited it to sit down and have a conversation about my new belief. I accepted what was in this moment and I trusted that I was where I needed to be at this time. Life was providing an opportunity for new growth.

It takes time to grow an empire, declares the Ruler archetype. Patience was a welcome energy as I settled into the trust and divine timing that God had a plan for me to attain even more.

Shadow Side of Money

One of my all-time favorite poems was written by Marianne Williamson, in her book, *A Return to Love*. I was in my late twenties when I first heard it, and it sent shivers throughout my entire body. It spoke to me on a deep soul level, as it addresses our potential and the power of God.

> *"Our deepest fear is not that we are inadequate. Our deepest fear is that we are powerful beyond measure. It is our light, not our darkness that most frightens us. We ask ourselves, 'Who am I to be brilliant, gorgeous, talented, fabulous?' Actually, who are you not to be? You are a child of God. Your playing small does not serve the world. There is nothing enlightened about shrinking so that other people won't feel insecure around you. We are born to shine, as children do. We were born to make manifest the glory of God that is within us. It is not just in some of us, it's in everyone. And as we let our own light shine, we unconsciously give other people permission to do the same. As we are liberated from our own fears, our presence automatically liberates others".*

Money was the final catalyst that brought this message home for me. The shadow side of money relationships is the part that keeps us in a place of fear. In my search for financial freedom, I discovered beliefs hidden beneath the surface that showed up in everyday blind spots, creating energy leaks within me and in my bank account. Energy leaks make our vessels dirty and block the connection with the source. I was confused about everything that had happened to me in the fall of the year. When I asked God to help me understand he pointed me to Wayne Dyer, *The Power of Intention*. Wayne described connecting to the source as reaching up and holding on to the trolly strap, which is something I have always done. To be in co-creation where I am inspired to create and allow spirit to move through my words requires trust and patience. In an open loving state, I find the pathways to make this possible. Immediately after, I set my intention for this book. I stepped into co-creation, and the words began to flow. To stay in union with my body, mind, and spirit, I took breaks to walk in nature, dance, and meditate.

The repeating pattern that showed up on the shadow side of my money relationships was twofold: my spending or overinvesting in my business, and expending resources without the influx of cash flow. Another way of saying this would be I gave my energy and attention to things I shouldn't have. It was a calling to learn patience, lean into waiting, and trust that this or something better will come if it is meant to be.

When I shared with my friend about working at the bank, she was thrilled. She mentioned feeling bad for my husband because he had wanted me to work at the bank, and I refused to do it. I reminded her and myself that was not the only reason we parted. I was now glad to be free of my marriage as hindsight revealed I was not respected or my feelings valued by him, or by myself. Being able to experience affection with my next partner made me realize just how much my love language had not been met. There was so much more for me in my life, and I still had more to explore about it.

My celebrity-archetype-sacred-money contract was to accumulate wealth while being admired and valued in the world. When our marriage ended, my husband would not stop saying how I added no financial value to our relationship. I may not have been an equal contributor monetarily, but he couldn't see my heart's desires or my efforts to try. His lack of seeing value in me was not in alignment with the value I had found within myself. In my first marriage, sex was a big desire, but it didn't matter if I wanted it or not. He didn't care if I cried during intercourse, he didn't see my value, and neither did I. I gave willingly of myself even when I didn't want it, or it was taken from me against my will. With my second husband, his desire for sex was not as strong as mine and he often rejected me. While it created conflict within me at first because of my attraction to him, I learned to go deeper inside myself, and not seek approval from him through sex. Later I learned how conditional his love was for me.

My celebrity archetype has an inner big shot who wants to illuminate, have a positive impact, and achieve recognition. Those components need to be found on the inside first and cannot be obtained through material or worldly possessions. My business includes plenty of visibility and makes a big impression, and for me, that means being authentic, not fake. I was not good at pretending to be a *fake it until I made it* kind of girl. I am sure I often projected an image of wealth that was not always consistent with my bank account. Now that image of wealth shines from within regardless of the balance in the bank account.

People tend to judge people by whether they are wealthy or poor. Let that go! Instead, see the value in people first and practice being more kind. Avoid hanging out with negative or judgmental people.

As a leader, I enjoy helping others endeavor to make a great impression on their lives and businesses. I love to inspire, and I am eager to support others with words or other resources. I enjoy standing out in a crowd and do so by being in alignment with my magnetic, confident, and radiant strengths.

I spent a large part of my life struggling and I did not shine. Instead, I hid and played small. I was insecure and struggled with depression. I lacked any confidence in who I was as a mother, wife, and woman. Thankfully, those days are behind me. Those moments when I would hit the wall and feel like it might be easier to end my life than meet the challenges before me were frightening. I know, though, it's not my life I want to end; it's the struggle. Having the tools to get to the core of that struggle helps. My desire to live a prosperous life is strong. How much I love, accept, and believe in myself has been priceless. I have discovered what true prosperous living entails. With this clearer understanding and the ability to break patterns, I began to study sacred money archetypes and gain an understanding of the universal language.

Archetypes

Each of us has the qualities of all the archetypes. For me, the "ruler" is the most dominant. The ruler is here to illuminate the desire to achieve. That desire is illuminated by my willingness to change and do the work to make it happen. The ruler wants to build an empire where everyone thrives, but feelings of not being enough and being out of alignment with the soul's highest potential prevent this. We were born enough; however, life experiences, especially regarding money or relationships, teach us to block our birthright of abundance. "Not enough" harms our level of worth.

You will not feel worthy if you feel you are not enough, which impacts your sense of self-esteem and your purpose, causing an imbalance in the root, sacral, and solar plexus chakras and making these chakras overwork. I recall asking Joe if he thought creating wealth meant giving it all your time and attention, even at the sacrifice of a relationship, and he agreed that in his situation yes, he did. However, perhaps building your empire is more important, and if you desire both a healthy relationship and a successful business, then you can create those too.

When my husband announced that he did not support my business, it triggered my fear of losing my identity, my wealth, and my control. I had finally found a career I loved and was passionate about and didn't want to lose it. Accumulating financial resources can create a sense of safety and protection from danger, which is an external comfort that is necessary for survival in our world. I know someone who took their life because of financial losses. Others have felt this way, struggling with deep wounds that block them from achieving financial success. I have to ask, *is it worth ending a life over money*? What would it look like in times of struggle if you turned inward and asked, *what do I need right now*? What if you lean into faith and prayer or your inner guide who is forever present waiting for you to reach up or go within?

Money is nothing without you.

This awareness shifted for me when I had no money or possessions, and yet inside, I felt completely safe and protected because I had complete trust in a higher power. I had a conversation with my daughter who said she was so happy to learn and embody this work because money used to create great anxiety within her. Now, she feels relaxed no matter the balance in her bank account. An inner connection with spirit can provide a sense of inner peace that cannot be bought. For years I never felt satisfied, always striving to achieve higher financial goals, but my deeply rooted belief of not being enough robbed me of joy and was an incredible liability. I thrive when my message helps to empower others, and I love to enrich lives through my business and personal life. It's also important to create an impact by demonstrating that I am thriving first. Not balancing my financial risk or energy was not thriving. I believed what I was creating was going to give me greater wealth in the future which often caused me to overwork. I gave all my attention to work and not as much to my relationships, which had a negative impact. Another important thing I witnessed was that when I stopped chasing money, it became easier for me to acquire it. I received clients organically during my sabbatical in the mountainous BC town. It was the law of attraction at play. Put another way, I see it as God supporting me because I was in alignment. I believe I was supported during this time of healing by the hand of God.

Being decisive is something I had to learn through practice. I enjoy creating, being innovative, and building growth opportunities. Being wishy-washy and indecisive does not work when you are building a business. Being indecisive meant I did not trust myself or God. I was told, "Make a decision, and stick with it, Janet." Instead, I would regret the decisions I made and believe I could do better. To break this pattern, I learned to decide from an empowered place. When I empowered my choices, I felt I was doing my best, and doing my best each day was important to me. These acts strengthened my trust and left me feeling more empowered as a woman, which bettered my life and business. I was connected to a powerful force and felt unstoppable in these moments. My writing coach for this book acknowledged that I chose to begin again, even when it could have been easy to quit. I am unable to quit. This force, my spirit within me, is too powerful. Some said it was an addiction; however, I know the truth and that is what matters to me. Being intuitively led by spirit might seem crazy to someone who does not engage with their spiritual self. Yes, at times I have questioned my sanity; however, my life and spiritual experiences are very real. And I am sane. The definition of insanity is doing the same thing over and over, expecting different results. I believe it is living proof that my results in life are different from anyone else's in my family lineage.

The maverick archetype in me is the inner rebel who does not cave easily to the opinions of others. I have become an independent thinker, and I encourage you to be as well. There is so much freedom when you can think and make empowered choices for yourself. I made so many decisions for the sake of others, the men in my life specifically, and I am happy to be breaking free of that pattern. It feels good to be a single woman. Freedom is a value of mine, and breaking the chains, be they beliefs or patterns, is how to access ultimate freedom. Just being attracted to getting rich can initiate the squirrel syndrome or shiny object syndrome, always looking everywhere for the answers or taking too many courses. At the beginning of my business, I was looking for someone else to tell me what to do to be successful, which led me to overinvest, which tipped the balance, and I risked financial stability.

If or when this happens, you may have to compromise to get through it (i.e. take a temporary job). I was always willing to take the risk for a potential big win, but that didn't always serve me well. When I ran out of financial resources in the past, I would be devastated. Over time my views of money became less important; it impacted me less emotionally as I leaned into the trust and guidance of spirit. I've learned to be patient and allow my asks to be answered with divine timing. This is where my high expectations often got me into trouble.

I would pay attention to the upside and the downside of the numbers; however, I still took too much risk.

Working with archetypes helps us fully understand the role that our emotions play and how our energy is impacted. Being on an emotional rollercoaster is not exciting. It means being out of balance. The lows would feel too low, and the highs would lead to impulsive spending. Paying attention to the numbers with emotional intelligence leads to much more happiness by creating awareness in the present on a higher frequency, rather than reacting from a place of fear or having something to prove. The maverick may always be looking at how to gain a financial win, but what is the fuel for this drive: greed, not having enough, or insecurities? Not creating from a place of love means erasing the possibility of alignment or creating from within to attain a higher power.

Napoleon Hill in his book, *Think and Grow Rich*, writes that we are in one of two states at all times – either love or fear. We must pay attention to our internal driver, our center of creation, so it will fuel our courage and develop the tenacity to create income from an empowered place within us, as well as fueling more grace and ease. In Matthew 6:24 echoes this sentiment with the words, "No one can serve two masters. Either you will hate one and love the other, or you will be devoted to one and despise the other. You can not serve both God and Money."

I kept a secret from my husband. I didn't tell him I created debt to build my business and when he found out, he was angry, and he had every right to be. As a reminder, I created a contract in the very early days of our relationship when I said, "You manage your money, and I will manage my money."

I know there is no integrity in being deceptive. I always prided myself on being honest, even saying that telling lies goes against my religion. Being untruthful is not the key to happiness. If I feel I must lie, then I am living in fear. Telling the truth, regardless of the reaction of another, keeps us in alignment and free of fear. Speaking the truth from a loving compassionate place is always easier to receive. We will get back what we give so we need to act in loving ways toward everyone. A common blind spot for people is to hide what they spend from their partner. They avoid having money conversations about creating debt to invest in a business, as I did. Couples who sleep together should have money conversations. I am afraid to say I created a contract against this at the beginning of our relationship. It is healthy to support one another with each other's dreams and goals. This is something I've read about, although I haven't experienced it so far. Many women I have spoken with feel that there is a double standard allowing the man to spend what he wants when he wants, while many women keep secret the resentment this makes them feel. Resentment in a relationship will create a division, first within yourself and then between the couple. When you are driven by unconscious fears, you are gambling with your financial security.

Spiritual entrepreneurs can be too much in the spiritual realm and not sufficiently manage what is happening in the physical. Too many individuals avoid structuring financial deals or handling financial complexities and wonder why they are not wealthy yet. This is worth repeating, denial is not the strategy for success and it's not keeping you real. When you focus your energy and talents on creating a sustainable income, you create a financial foundation that frees you to engage in new and exciting opportunities. This puts you in the higher vibrational states of joy, love, prosperity, and abundance. Breathe that in. Regulate your body and allow peace to fill you.

The Accumulator archetype is here to illuminate respect and appreciation. If you are not respecting yourself, don't expect to receive respect from others. Men who knew me growing up now message me about how much respect they have for me as a woman, yet when I was younger, that was not the case. They didn't respect me, they only wanted one thing from me, and I know it was a result of my lack of self-respect. Now, that I have more respect for myself, I no longer tolerate the things I once did. I have healthy boundaries around how I want the men in my life to treat me. I see myself as being sacred.

We are all sacred, so why not have healthy, clear boundaries and self-respect? We are as good as the credit we give to ourselves. T. Harv Eker writes in his book *Secrets of the Millionaire Mind*, "How we do money is how we do everything." If you tend to judge others based on money habits, you will judge yourself with the same standards. Or you may be denying your habits, perhaps not directly but in a relationship with yourself or others. Going against your truth or higher self is not a sign of respect or appreciation. Feeling anxious, worried, or greatly reluctant to spend money means you are in the lower-frequency playground. Look closer if you are being obsessive, or compulsive about your emotions, thoughts, or actions with money. Having a busy, money-monkey mind is not a quiet mind that welcomes higher intuitive insights. Lack of trust in money may also be a sign that you lack trust in God, or you doubt your own belief that you can create what you want in life or, even better, allow the will of God to create through you. Even if you can save easily and create financial independence, if a lack of self-worth is your driver, then the size of your bank account doesn't matter. Being robbed of your self-worth can rob you of living in peace and harmony.

Guilt is an emotion that can rob you of joy at any moment. Some women feel guilty for investing in themselves. They feel guilty giving themselves self-care or spending money on themselves. They also feel guilty for not spending money. It is a vicious cycle. Here's the thing: *a healthy sense of guilt can let you know if you are going against what you value.* Let's say, you have set an intention to pay off your debt and then you dived into a spending detox. While your value was to be financially free and honor this commitment, instead you made credit card purchases, creating more debt, which made you feel guilty. You have just created an act *against* yourself. To correct the negative reaction, make a new choice to return an item or create the money *before* you make the purchase. Fearing that you will run out of money causes stress and anxiety, and I have known many accumulators with plenty of money who were afraid to invest in themselves, even if they intuitively felt the calling to do so. This worry about not spending even the smallest amounts, and not trusting that money is an unlimited resource, limits the potential for more abundance.

Abundance can come in more ways than money. It is everywhere. But you must relate to it internally by feeling it. Placing self-imposed limits upon yourself can prevent you from stretching and achieving the success you truly desire. If you are already skilled at money management, challenge yourself to apply your energy and talents to create greater wealth, allowing yourself to be open to opportunities of abundance and better able to serve others.

Ask yourself if past experiences are limiting you from achieving greater levels of happiness in other areas of your life or relationships. Notice the moments when you are hesitant to invest in yourself or when you are judging others. Can you find acceptance in all people without judgment or blame? Have you found acceptance within yourself and for all the parts of you that are equally good and bad?

Connector archetypes may have plenty of faith and optimism but if they do not see the value within themselves, they may feel disconnected internally and avoid growing in relationships. They tell themselves they do not like people or avoid sharing their gifts and talents with certain classes of people. Connection internally is important and if this piece is missing it will be mirrored in your outer world. Lacking financial independence may cause you to lean on another too much, or perhaps you lack trust and confidence in your abilities. You might not be overly stressed around money, but you might also avoid managing your money because when you do, the sense of being overwhelmed is too much for you to handle. This is not the pathway to success or achieving happiness. Your strength is to trust, but in this sense, are you trusting someone else and not yourself or your connection with the source?

T. Harv Eker also wrote that the universe will not give you more money if you cannot handle the money you have. Ask yourself: If you avoid money challenges, are you also in the habit of avoiding emotions or challenging conversations? When we grow up without healthy role models around money, we may be trapping ourselves in disempowering patterns that prevent us from discovering ways we can heal. Starting fresh means taking responsibility for learning how to make healthy financial choices for yourself and taking action to learn financial management skills. This can be extremely empowering as you rise from lower vibrations of shame and embarrassment to feeling more empowered and inspired. This opens you to more creativity and allows you to be more innovative in your wealth creation. Educating yourself and taking care of your own financial needs moves you forward, fully in alignment and empowered.

On the other hand, having faith that you will always be taken care of without taking physical action to empower your money relationships puts you and your loved ones in jeopardy. You and only you are responsible for your mental, emotional, physical, and financial well-being. Your lack of boundaries is not someone else's fault.

Being a part of a community or having individuals who support you is also important. Consider what happens when a relationship is lost through death or divorce or even having a partner who fails to support you in some of these areas. How you react can leave you feeling depleted and compromise your health. You might sink into blaming and feel resentful towards God, yourself, or your partner for your situation. To get your power back, you must accept what was your responsibility and acknowledge the ways you may have given away your power.

Forgiveness is extremely healing. I often guide my clients to the ho'oponopono prayer, as it is extremely helpful in letting go of what no longer serves you. It takes you to a peaceful place within yourself. For example, focus your attention on someone you feel you have given too much of yourself to or behaved in ways that disempowered you. See them in your mind's eye and repeat, *I love you, I forgive you, I thank you, and I am sorry*. Notice where you might feel any resistance or heaviness and keep going until you feel a release. You might try journaling about your emotions which can help to clear or transform old wounds and negative feelings. Permit yourself to be honest in expressing your emotions on paper. I have heard women say they once journaled, and someone read it, so they no longer feel safe doing so. I understand, this happened to me when my first husband found and read all my journals. Still, I encourage you to keep writing and scribble over the words if you must make it unreadable to another. Eventually, when you feel completely safe in who you are, you will not hesitate to share your deepest thoughts with others you feel safe with.

 I did this with Joe one morning. He asked me to share what I'd written in my journal. He was surprised when I was happy to share with him exactly what I had written. I am open in my life, as I no longer choose to live in fear. If you are angry, let yourself express the emotions of anger to move the energy through you. Keeping your feelings bottled up does not serve you. If you are lying to yourself by stuffing away your emotions, you will not find the freedom you are seeking, financially or otherwise. You will find happiness when you are managing your money and your emotions by making decisions for yourself, rather than relying on someone else or avoiding what is your responsibility. If you are a connector archetype, you care about heart-to-heart connections.

So, when you empower your relationship within yourself and see your value, it shifts you towards a deeper connection within yourself—your enlightened self. You cannot give to others what you have yet to integrate within yourself. Others will trigger what you need to see about yourself. It's important to not let your current circumstances define you or stop you from taking the right actions toward creating your financial independence. Each day provides us with a new opportunity to create a life more on our terms. It is important to let go of sinking into victim-like feelings by shaming or blaming yourself. You are capable and you are enough right now.

Romantic archetypes are the pleasure seekers who enjoy the pleasures of life. Patterns such as flamboyant spending, ignoring/denying, or avoiding anything to do with money are a shadow part of this archetype that can compromise the ability to create financial freedom and enjoy life to its fullest. Underneath you may feel undeserving, unappreciated, or even unloved, and you might mask the feelings with these patterns. Take the mask off and allow yourself to heal these wounds. You will feel freer on the inside. Then take action to make yourself and your financial situation healthy. I've had clients deny that they are romantics and are resistant to unlocking the doors to true abundance, even though their strengths are pleasure-seeking, and feeling luxurious. They use their energy to create wholeness and self-worth from the inside out, and tap into a more meaningful life that money can not buy. If you are a romantic, you must find ways to achieve pleasure by not spending money. You do this by tapping into your creations and embracing new ideas that leave you feeling more fulfilled. When you spend and say,

"I deserve this," are you comprising your financial security by creating more debt? Perhaps you love giving gifts, or when you say no to yourself you encounter resistance. Tap into your emotional triggers, as they are gifts to help you learn more about yourself. Believing there will always be more and being generous with others are your gifts; however, if you keep sacrificing yourself through overindulging, you will ultimately rob yourself of your truest sense of self-worth and the security of achieving financial freedom. When you avoid making money changes with your behaviors, even when you know it will benefit you, realize that you are compromising your financial well-being. Life is meant to be enjoyed, and saving money is healthy for you. You might dream of living a more luxurious life but if you keep indulging in over-giving and avoiding taking responsibility for your money because you feel inadequate, then you risk feeling unsatisfied or resentful. Those are not good feelings, as they tend to keep your frequency in a lower state. Embrace creating financial security and live your life to its fullest, inside and out.

The Alchemist archetypes are role models for positive change. Their inner idealist will pull them more toward the shadow sides when they feel a love-hate relationship with money. They may even be attracted to earning money in unconventional ways, such as healing, social justice, and leading causes. The energy of hate and feelings of unfairness around wealth prevents them from creating the wealth required to do better in the world. This is where they find themselves leaning on others for financial support, which makes them feel vulnerable. They may be insecure about their ability to create income to support the causes they care about. Not having the money to support their causes or thrive in business leaves them feeling unhappy, as if they are not using their talents to their fullest potential. Becoming self-aware of these limiting attitudes around money can help them shift from fear to transforming many of their amazing ideas into financial success. They often find it easy to empower others to believe in themselves but fail to embody the same belief within themselves. The alchemist may rebel against or feel resistant to creating money goals or habits that would support them. Instead, they rely on others and feel overly judgmental about money. The cycle of overthinking feels like a madness that is real until they begin focusing their energy on monetizing their ideas, which of course has the power to impact others in amazing ways.

Ask yourself this question, *If money were sacred, how would you treat it*? Now, look in the mirror for a deeper reflection. You are sacred. How are you treating yourself? What about your thoughts, are they predominately positive or negative? Are you loving yourself more than you hate yourself? What about your beliefs, are they in alignment with creating the ideas that are being gifted to you? Start by championing yourself, then turn your ideas into practical actions that transform and inspire both you and others.

The Nurturer archetype is extremely caring and compassionate but can put others' needs ahead of their own. This can be self-sacrificing and disempowering. Nurturers appreciate money but feel they have to over-give, or perhaps allow themselves to be taken advantage of in relationships. They may feel the need to rescue others. If you are a Nurturer, stop feeling bad for others and begin to feel for yourself. Healthy people feel. Being giving, devoted, and reliable doesn't mean you have to sacrifice yourself for the benefit of others. Permit yourself to say no to people who are using you or taking advantage of you financially or otherwise. Ask yourself, why you are staying in a relationship that is not making you happy. Is it because you are not loving yourself enough? Is there an unhealed place within you that feels afraid to be alone or vulnerable? Look at those moments when you are satisfying the needs of others over your own or where you might be abandoning yourself. Let go of being a martyr. Your job is not to heal someone else. Giving can take many different forms, including healthy boundaries and being able to tell someone "No, what you are doing is hurting me and that is not okay." Acknowledge that you cannot change others, and yes, people need support, but so do you. Support yourself and your relationships by empowering yourself. Creating clear boundaries is a very powerful way for you to demonstrate compassion. Be a role model by turning care and compassion toward yourself. Extend grace to yourself where past experiences or wounds may still be holding you back from living a life that feels fulfilling and whole to you. Be your inner sponsor and grow your sense of self-worth. Many of my clients are excellent givers but not so great at receiving. This is where deeper work is required to identify and move through the challenges of the negative patterns that are holding them back.

Not acknowledging our shadow side leaves us living in the ego or fear side of self. I use fear and ego as the same word. Remember that none of it is bad. It's a part of being human and it is important to love all the parts of who we are. If we are blind to our faults, then we could be judging others, living more like a hypocrite, and feeling very unsatisfied in relationships. That's okay if we're happy where we are in life and do not want to change. Each of us will grow to the extent that we want to or feel called to by our inner spirit.

If you don't see your ego, you may project your beliefs and negative thoughts onto others, telling yourself you have all the answers, finding fault, and being quick to tell people what you feel is wrong about them. In my experience when I think I know a lot, life will quickly remind me how little I know. Occasionally, You may think you are right, and the rest of the world is screwed up, but not you. You have it all figured out. This, my friend, is a sense of superiority and ego at its finest. Ego loves to be right. It loves to point fingers at others rather than taking a closer inventory of liabilities that rob you of loving and living life to its fullest. Be mindful of these ego traps. If you are in a relationship where the other person is not willing and open to change, leave and don't look back.

"Remember that love is patient, love is kind. It does not envy, it does not boast, it is not proud. It does not dishonor others, it is not self-seeking, it is not easily angered, and it keeps no records of wrongs" (1 Corinthians 13).

It is not your job to heal or fix anyone except yourself, but if required, make a choice. If you don't feel you need healing, and that you are happy with who you are, then life will feel good for you. Celebrate who you are and continue loving and living life to its fullest. Be open and set healthy boundaries for yourself. Remember you see the world through your lens which is made up of your own stories, motivations, and fears. Love, love, and more love are the solution, and opening yourself up by being a witness to the fearful sides of yourself and others will put you in a position of empowerment, not superiority. It will raise your level of consciousness. You can give yourself full permission to access the power of co-creation and live life more on your terms, rather than being driven by ego or someone else's needs. When you are grounded in who you are, you can enter any negative or challenging situation and remain at peace within yourself. You will no longer be impacted by negative attitudes, energy, or projections from others.

A cycle of completion has come full circle for me at this time in my life. I am proud of how far I have come. I celebrate this and breathe deeply, reflecting on the journey it took to get here. It required a lot of work, and I am excited about what my future will hold. As for new relationships, my focus is on me and my purpose, which is to share my gifts and talents in this world. When the timing is right, I will accept and choose a partner who accepts all of me; I will settle for nothing less. I love myself and I am so worthy of living this prosperous life.

>Breathe deep.
>I honor the place in you that is the same as in me.
>I honor the place from which you have come.
>The universe provides.
>I honor the place in you of peace and truth.
>I honor the place in you that is fearful or feeling insecure.
>I honor the place in you that is the same in me.
>There is but one.
>Namaste

You are Empathic

The day arrived when I would begin my career with RBC. Days prior, a friend asked if I was excited, and I said no. I rose in the morning and practiced yoga, meditation, and danced. I wanted to prepare and be grounded for my day. As I soaked in the bath, an anxious energy began to move through me. I witnessed the fear growing more intense as I got closer to the time to leave for work.

I dropped Leo, my dog, off at my friend's house. My insides were in turmoil. I did not want to go. I turned my car around and stopped in a parking lot to pray. *Trust me* were the words I heard.

My resistance caused me to arrive late, which is unlike me as I always arrive on time. I gave myself permission to show up and see what the day would bring. The manager was not in, which left me without access to the training I was to begin that day. I got re-acquainted with a few old colleges and spent the day at the front entrance welcoming clients on a busy Monday. I stood in a place of being a witness for myself and others.

At the end of the day during my drive home, my daughter called to see how my day went. I cried. My heart opened and tears poured out. She offered me words of support and I was so overwhelmed that I had to let her go. I continued to cry for hours later and when my girlfriend called, I thought I may have lost my mind. She knew better. I cried at the deep realization that my return to the bank was because I gave my energy to Joe, rather than my business. I did not want to be there and was afraid I would lose freedom through corporate restriction and that it would limit the flexible time I had found in my life for my practice. I cried myself to sleep that night, waking suddenly at 3:00 a.m.

You are an empath. were the words shouting at me. My God, I am empathic. It was clear to me I'd never realized the depth of what this meant. My heart had been opened, and I could easily take on the emotional energy of others. It is what makes me good at my job as a soulful money coach. I have experienced this many times over the years; however, with the work I get to do and expanding my consciousness, I feel everything that much deeper. I always knew my intuitive ability was strong and being connected to this piece of the puzzle helped me understand myself on another level.

I did not return to banking as a career. The events that followed would lead me to go deeper, almost losing myself, only to return home again with a deeper realization.

I want to remind you that you are on a journey of self-discovery. It is truly infinite, how far we can expand our perceptions. Remember, this is a process. Be gentle as you fold away every layer to get to know yourself and understand the role of your emotions in your life. Before I share my experience, I want to remind you what love is.

"Love is patient, love is kind. It does not envy, it does not boast, it is not proud. It does not dishonor others, it is not self-seeking, it is not easily angered, and it keeps no records of" wrongs (1 Corinthians 1).

Remember to extend this love to yourself above all else. You must love yourself more in times of conflict and inner struggle, as it will bring you home to yourself when all feels lost.

I waited for my next sign. Confused and conflicted, I did not have the energy my work required so I stepped back from doing what I felt passionate about. It was as if I and my money relationship were falling apart. I sat in stillness for months, waiting for the spirit to give me a sign. I knew I had to go to work. I knew I did not want to be in the cold northern climate. I knew too many things happened in this city, and I did not want to be here.

The message would come in a dream. I stood at the base of a mountain and someone I did not know was up above shooting arrows down at me. There was a river near the mountains that I floated down and I remember feeling safe.

Within days, I reached out to a girlfriend who lived on Vancouver Island. She shared her thoughts that I was an island girl, and the North was not the place for me. She said, "You should come here. There is a lot of work and it's a good place to figure things out." She sent me a picture of the mountain in front of her house: Arrow Smith Mountain. The town had a little river. This was my sign and I prepared to move. I left behind my furniture, and my library of books, everything that would not fit in the back of my truck. My child agreed to take care of Leo until I could send for him.

I left for the island, stopping along the way for a visit with Joe. We were not in a relationship and my move was for me, not him. I spent the night with him and headed out. I was nervous and excited to begin this journey and stand on my own two feet.

I wanted things in my life to be easy. I had been through enough challenges, so I looked for part-time work that would allow me time to do my business when I was ready. Arriving on the island, I walked down the street of Qualicum and it felt good. I wanted to work here. I breathed in the ocean air and felt the energy of both harmony and expansion.

Within the first week, I received a job at the local natural food health store as a cashier and another position at a barn doing chores. The work was easy; however, it took my body time to adjust to the challenges of standing all day at the store and the physical work of the barn chores. Time to adjust to changes is required in many areas of our life.

During w eek two, Joe announced he did not want to lose me and was coming to the island to buy a house. My spare time once again was given to Joe and not my work. Together we explored much of the island but did not find a suitable house. My part-time work and wages were not providing me with enough income to pay my debts. I was facing another bankruptcy.

I interviewed for an intern role as a branch manager at a bank. I knew the income would change the direction I was heading. I made it to stage two of the interview process. Joe presented me with an alternative solution. If I did not get this position, I could move in with him; we could work together and take our relationship to the next level. Things were happening so quickly, I barely had time to think. A part of me wanted to move in with Joe. At the moment, the bank emailed to say they selected another candidate; Joe and I were thrilled. I left the island after six weeks.

During those six weeks, my outer world continued to amaze me. I loved the lakes and mountains. I embraced my new work and discovered how to do things that I had no idea I was capable of. Physically my body grew stronger, and so did my bank account. I became so busy that I hardly had time for even a ten-minute practice in the morning. In the beginning, my mindset was strong as I enjoyed my new environment. However not having my practice impacted me negatively, and as the weeks passed, I became more emotionally unstable and disconnected from my spirit and purpose.

When I first moved in, Joe created space in a separate house in another town for me to do yoga, and it was in this space that I left what few valuables I had kept. In the house where we spent the majority of our time due to work, I recall telling a friend that there was no space for my intelligence or spirituality. Once again, I failed to recognize my mistake. Since the beginning of my relationship with Joe, I limited who I am. I lacked any boundaries and did not even realize what I needed to keep me feeling in harmony. I easily sacrificed things that were important to my well-being. Why did I not see what was so sacred to me? How could I let it go so easily? I had yet to realize the impact of this. I was separating myself from what was most important to me. There was a cost, as well as a reward.

I believe that we create our reality, and what we think about is how we feel. We use our emotions and energy to create or manifest what we want. I shut the door on myself, and I took full responsibility for what unfolded; however, it would take me to an even deeper understanding of myself and what I needed to see on a subconscious level. I blame no one, as that would only give away my power. Right now, I am in the process of taking it back, one day at a time as I step out of living in denial.

Returning Home

I am writing this final Chapter in the northern town where I have returned to stay with my girlfriend. I arrived stripped down, left with nothing, yet knowing that I have everything I need within me.

My relationship with Joe was confusing and chaotic from the very beginning. From the energy that I felt in my chakras, to our exploration of sex, adventure, joy, punishment, lies, and control. Moving in with Joe, I got to see a side of him I knew was a deep love. I had huge respect for him because he created so much abundance. He took responsibility and managed it with grace and ease. He thrived in his life. I knew when he asked me to move in with him, it was not a decision he made lightly. He chose me and wanted me to live in his world. He opened the door to trust which was something that had been broken in previous relationships. His views of women were that they were manipulative from the beginning of time. Joe was kind and fair to his employees, gentle with his friends, and worked with great effort to achieve his wealth. In my eyes, he was the definition of prosperous. He admitted he was hard on me at times and that his fears would cause him to be controlling. In the end, Joe taught me to stand in my power. He taught me to see my value and worth. He showed me that I was capable of creating the life I wanted through my efforts. I loved sides of him and yet there was another side that triggered great fear in me, and that fear would teach me what I was not seeing about my life. I became highly emotional, and I found myself crying too much and would be startled easily by sudden noises. My inner world was shaken.

I enjoyed life with Joe, but too often I would shrink back and not speak up in moments that were creating harm for me. In the moments where I did speak up, he was immediately sorry, as he recognized his actions were causing harm. Together we found a solution that would be more harmonious for both of us at work. Managing the intensity that came with the jobs, employees, and tenants was not what Joe intended to press upon me. I found myself navigating through it all and my mindset was strong as I rose to face the challenges. Yet inside, I began to feel insecure and retreat into fear. Joe would tease me relentlessly and I often felt devalued, and when I told him, he sat across from me and said that was not his intention and he was deeply sorry. He admitted that his teasing me was a way of expressing love. He knew I was sensitive, and I am sure it was a challenge for him, but these were behaviors I needed him to change. A little teasing is okay. I am playful and love to tease as well; however if teasing gets to the point where it robs you of your self-esteem, then it becomes unhealthy in a relationship.

Joe was opening the door to plan our future together. Retirement was coming and we were planning what that was going to look like. I wanted our life together and yet I was growing insecure and afraid. I was afraid of doing something that would end our relationship based on Joe's controlling behaviors. Joe let me know with his words there were many things I could potentially do that could threaten our relationship or cause it to end. But that was his fear of showing up. He also said that I could do anything and that he would never leave me, that he was excited to have me as a life partner. My body began to freeze in fear, and I had to work hard to orgasm when we had sex. I went to buy a new bra only to feel insecure and not confident enough to make a decision. I went to purchase a bikini. I asked the clerk if they had a modest swimsuit and she looked me in the eye and asked me if I was shy. I purchased a one-piece suit that might have been more suitable for a much older lady and left the store.

Who am I? What had I become? I used to be empowered, sexy, confident, and full of love. I used to be free. I no longer felt free. I was afraid and was living in fear. I was completely aware of its looming presence.

We had one week of calm, a bad tenant left, work was flowing smoother, and Joe was heading out of town without me. I told myself I was worthy of a man like Joe and that he deserved to have a woman like me.

I knew what I was about to do would get me into trouble. But I did not stop myself. I needed to release some pressure or run from myself. At the end of my workday, I joined our new neighbor downstairs for some drinks. She was a hippy-momma-bear kind of woman, and I drank too much wine and we danced. I love to dance. We had a moment when I was talking about my mother's cancer when she hugged me. She had lost her mother a year or two prior. When she hugged me, I hugged her hard and I cried from the depths of my soul. I did not know how much I needed the embrace or the love. At 2:30 am I woke to use the washroom and I received a text from Joe.

"I feel like you fucked up."

I lied "No, I did not. I spent the evening with the neighbor and had some drinks." He was aware days before that she invited me down. "Did you dance?"

"YES, I did."

In Joe's eyes, I did something very disrespectful. He felt it was sneaky and deceitful. He arrived home on Sunday night and made it clear he needed time to process what I had done. I gave him space. I asked him if he wanted me to leave. He said, no. He asked me to take time to reflect on my behavior. So, I wrote a letter about my emotions leading up to the event and why I behaved in such a disrespectful way.

Things would spiral out of control between us. Everything that happened would trigger more fear in me and my body went into flight mode. I did not think, and I reacted irrationally. Fear will do that. Joe's fears triggered my core wound of abandonment and I felt everything he did following that night and several days ahead was to punish me. It was not his intention, but his actions showed me differently; it was my perception in a heightened state of what was happening in those moments.

Joe arrived home before me. The day had not been good for me. I arrived to find him resting so I headed out to the lake for a swim. Joe had been teaching me to dive and today, unlike any other day I had no hesitation as I confidently dove in the water and swam as far as I could out into the lake. Something inside me felt stronger and things were about to change.

Joe was ready to talk about my letter. I felt the conversation was immature; Joe felt we had reached an understanding. I felt my choices were being limited. Our fears were dividing us. I felt stripped down.

The next day, we woke early as usual. Joe got ready for the day, and I realized I had more than enough time for a twenty-minute practice. I needed to reset. Once I was finished, I was surprised to find Joe ready to leave without me. He gave me instructions about what to do for the day and left me to drive myself to work. I felt again that he was punishing me.

I welcomed the extra time that I had and wrote down some goals I wanted to give attention to later. I left for work, hooking up the truck and trailer as I had several runs to make before I would meet Joe at the park. I had done this many times, but today it felt really hard. I said aloud, "It doesn't need to be this hard." I was feeling strange and had to ground myself often. Joe left out one piece of instruction, and I messaged him for clarity. He was irritated and told me to read my text, as he'd already instructed me on what to do. I said, "no you did not." He stated, "do not call me a liar." I asked him to re-read his message. When he did, he admitted his error. I went about my job only to find myself confused about where I needed to go. I had been down this road hundreds of times, yet I had to think hard about how to get there. My mind was empty. I could not remember how to get to my destination. Joe messaged to say he wanted freedom in our relationship and a few other things.

"Do you want me to leave?" I texted.

His response was "You can make that choice, Janet."

The message I received internally was, *You can leave, Janet. You can make that choice and not have to be told to leave.*

I returned to the shop and broke down in tears. I had to make a decision.

"Joe, I'm going to finish up this job, go home, take my uninsured truck that hasn't been picked up by the bailiff yet, pack my things and leave."

"You are running again. Stop."

I told him, "Yes, I am running from you, and I have every right to."

I am sharing this episode with you in limited detail to respect Joe's privacy. Being with him meant I would discover the most empowering lesson of my life. Sensitive, kind, loving, and generous, Joe also had his darkness and could misuse power. Truly, we all have dualities. We are human. Our perceptions of the events that unfolded between us are completely different. None of what I felt seemed true for him. He saw and felt things differently. Or he was as in denial as I was about the unhealthy parts of us. At the beginning of our relationship, Joe felt I was full of ego. People close to me would disagree. I am spiritual, kind, and loving. Joe did help me to see parts of my ego and helped me to become humbler. He helped me let go of what I thought I needed so I could embrace more and put my life in alignment once and for all. Before meeting Joe, I felt I was living life in alignment at a certain level, and that there was a pattern I needed to break. Joe was a powerful teacher, and he triggered the core wound of abandonment that was within me, which triggered my need to claim my birthright of power and value.

The problem was that I dimmed my light to be in the presence of Joe. Much like my husband, Joe did not like my celebrity archetype, which meant being visible, or my spiritual work as a healer. I lived my life by default falling into patterns and behaviors that did not serve my highest self.

On my ten-hour drive after leaving Joe, I had moments where I would ask myself, *Should I turn back?*

No, Keep going.

I felt guilty for leaving my job with Joe which provided me with a solid, consistent income. I was sorry for letting go of this responsibility. There was a moment when I heard a quiet voice inviting me to sit on the dock near the water, but I chose to ignore it. What if I had taken a seat, said a prayer, and asked for a miracle?

I told myself, *My mental, emotional, and spiritual well-being is worth more than a thirty-dollars-an-hour job.*

I drove at night, in the rain, through the smoke of the fires, arriving at my friend's home at 3:30 a.m. I was exhausted.

I was free.

Truth

The key to happiness is to live your truth. In my relationship with Joe, I had stopped living my truth. As a result, my soul was neglected, I was divided, and I became unhappy. My entire life, I wanted a relationship with God. I wanted to know him more than anything else in this world. I desired happiness, healthy relationships, and financial freedom. Joe and I never created a foundation for a healthy relationship. I tolerated all the flags and denied myself protection. I failed to hold the value in what I found in myself, and I lost what I didn't think I could. I am thankful the loss was only temporary, as I held onto my core values. When I am tempted to retreat to a place of insecurity, indecisiveness, and unhappiness, I ask myself,

Who am I?

I hear the answer.

I am love. I am light.

This brings me home to my heart. My heart is for God. Always was and forever will be. My entire life, I searched for love outside myself from my parents, men, and external experiences. My pursuit of money took me on a wild chase until I found what I'd been seeking .

The pivotal moment came when I was sitting quietly and felt the right and left sides of my brain come together. I knew I had connected to higher consciousness and God. I had healed my wound of not being enough, of not being safe and secure so that I could open my pathways to become one with spirit. I can ask questions and receive the answers. I am in a place of love more of the time. I am kind to myself. I don't hold myself hostage for my past mistakes. I am open and free for God to work through me. I feel it in my work as a prosperous woman financial coach, when I teach yoga, and in the expression of my writings. My gift is to teach. I teach love, truth, and freedom to those who seek love, truth, and freedom.

The change that had shifted in me took me to a place of enlightenment. I was honored. I knew my work mattered, and it filled me with spirit and purpose. I became happy in my life when I looked at my past experiences that previously left me feeling wounded, the ones that made me feel like there was something wrong with me. I was able to forgive myself. My perception shifted when I looked at each experience and discovered a different level of understanding of the circumstances, the people and their roles, and our shared woundedness. I found forgiveness which opened my heart to more love. As I expanded in love, I found more joy. I understood the power of my thoughts and changed them from being negative to more loving. I became healthy in mind and body which made room for spirit. I used the tools I was given to practice yoga, meditation, walking, journaling, and prayer daily.

Money can be a powerful influence. Intuition asked me *Will I trust my decisions, regardless of the money that is in my life? Am I serving money or GOD?* I was in service for money most of my life. My wants were self-driven. My money relationship taught me to go even deeper so that I could free myself from the fear of needing approval, the security of a man, of losing in relationships. The more work I did understanding my archetypes around money, the less motivated I was by money and the more I was motivated by God. I was lost; then I found myself. God's loving grace guided me back home. My question became, *How can I serve your will?*

Change and personal growth can feel threatening to those around us. My changes made others uncomfortable. My changes also helped others to grow by being willing and open. After experiencing my connection with God, I didn't think I could ever lose it, unless I get too busy "doing" or when I abandon my practices. When I do either of those things, I feel the all too familiar feeling of anguish in the depths of my soul.

There is so much to discover about ourselves. Could our true purpose on earth be to achieve our highest self and expression of love? Can we heal our wounds and no longer be triggered by negative experiences? Can we be aware and willing to take a look into those parts that still hurt and explore what is needed and wanted from *Ourselves*?

Joe and I had talked about working through our differences together and it felt good. I felt if I could be myself in the relationship, we could have it all. Joe didn't want a woman like me. He did not want to change and was not willing to go deeper. Neither did my husband, who declared I was no longer the woman he married, that I had changed, and he wanted his old wife back. So, I had choices to make to heal. I was ready. I prayed, *Dear God, please heal me.*

I've discovered that my core wound is abandonment. Throughout my life, I have attracted relationships with men who tuned into the instability I experienced growing up. In these men, I would abandon myself, repeatedly. I was attracted to strong men with power because they mirrored the strength and power that I so wanted to hold and express. This is why I have written *Heal Your Money, Heal Your Life: A Healing Guide for Freedom Seekers.*

How about you? Are you ready to rise and claim your power? Break the chains of your habits and embedded patterns. Rest if you must, but do not give up. It will be difficult. You may wish it weren't so hard. When you feel weak, lean into your higher power. Trust your strength, courage, and intuition. Be a great student and an even better teacher. You were born for this. Own your value, the worth of all you've learned and worked so hard to become. Serve from the heart center, and the money will show up because you are receiving and sending your energy differently. Your energy is currency. You have gifts. Do not hold back. You are the freedom seeker. You are seeking the freedom that comes from feeling whole and authentic. You are enough.

Epilogue

Last fall, in a dream, I heard the words, *Janet, you do not need to change anymore.* I felt that truth as I accepted and loved all of me, even though I was in a place of conflict and confusion. I went on to change myself in a relationship that was not for me. I had to create room for myself first. A therapist once asked me this question.

"Janet, do you love your father?"

"Yes, he's my father, of course, I love him."

What I failed to see was that the behaviors of my father were not based on love. The behaviors of violence, control, manipulation, and punishment are not of love. Those patterns and behaviors are ones of fear and darkness, actions based on my father's own wounds.

This common thread has been woven into all of my relationships with men. I had to strip it all down and let it go so that I could get to the core of who I am. I do not need to change now; however, I feel I will continue to grow and expand because I accept myself. I can no longer tolerate being in a relationship with someone who cannot accept all of me. I accept all of me.

I have felt shaken by all the events that occurred in my life. Along with hitting my yoga mat for slow practice each day, I decided I needed to go to a place where the energy of God would be spoken. I returned to church for guidance.

The message for me that day was *Do not fear. Trust God when he calls me to do something and be patient in the moments I have to wait.* God asks us to heal wounds created by fear-based experiences because he wants to give us more. He wants us to prosper and live heaven on earth. It is okay that we retreat to places of comfort; patterns will repeat themselves until we are ready for the next level.

Unfortunately, we live in a world that supports not-enoughness, a world that values money over people where fear is so strong that it is overwhelming and toxic for our spirits. I find myself asking *How will I navigate in this world of fear?* Love is the solution. Love is how I will navigate in this world. Love for myself and others.

With God's grace, I was guided to change my internal foundation. In doing so, my outer world changed. I began to make the right choices following the guidance I was given. Now I am ready to create from a different foundation. I will continue to lean into love, and everything will work out for me in miraculous ways. I experience the love that God has for me, and it is awe-inspiring. I will give myself time to reflect and receive it fully.

I encourage you to ask yourself: What is the state of your foundation? Do you need to rebuild? Pray to God to light the path and show you the way. Do you require healing? Ask for it. Are you happy?

Pray for the courage to change the parts within you that are creating this unhappiness. Let go of what is negative within you and pray for help to do so. Are you happy in your relationships? Do you desire freedom? Gently go deeper. Permit yourself to explore. Be honest with yourself and listen to your inner calling, as you are meant to. Let go of lies, punishments, control, and manipulation. Establish boundaries to protect yourself from those who want to inflict fear upon you, consciously or unconsciously. Become a better witness for yourself and others. Embrace more love, kindness, openness, forgiveness, and gentleness for yourself and others. Hold space for both Fear and Love that are within you and in the world.

This will take work, I know. Remember, you are capable. I do believe that what we do to heal on an individual level will impact the world in amazingly positive ways.

That day in church, two women and a baby were in front of me. I considered moving because I can sometimes get distracted by the cries of a baby but decided to stay. In a moment, the infant looked at me and extended her hand. I held it. It was a moment for me that symbolized the generations that are rising, and how they need people like me and you to be an anchor in love.

**"You are the light of the world.
A town on a hill cannot be hidden" (Matthew 5:14).**

MATTHEW 5:14

I received baptism as a Christian. I resonated with being a healer of one's spirit in my words, work, and life. I discovered my purpose is to heal and inspire others to do the same. I intend to continue to be an example of that. My ultimate purpose is to be my best self, giving and receiving authentic love.

I've written this book in the hope that, by sharing my heart and my story, you may find your truth. Go deeper to examine your integrity. Heal wounds so that you can become a whole human being. Remember what love is. This verse is worthy of repeating.

"Love is patient. Love is kind. It does not envy, it does not boast, it is not proud. It does not dishonor others, it is not self-seeking, and it keeps no records of wrongs " (1 Corinthians 13).

I am doing the work to break the chains forged by generations of my family. I have been called to do this. As I grew in love, as an empath, my sensitivity to fear heightened and had to be acknowledged. I discovered I can no longer tolerate relationships that make me shrink or live with a scarcity mindset. I can no longer allow myself to retreat. I accept all of me. In my spirit, I am perfect and whole. I build healthy boundaries and make choices that are right for me. I know myself more and I accept and love the woman, mother, and partner I have become. I leave room for mistakes as I heal and step into new levels of growth. My life had been filled with trauma. The impacts of emotional abuse created a foundation in me that needed to be unearthed so that I could plant seeds that would take root and blossom into a new life.

I am clear now more than ever. Clear about who I am as a woman and how I can be of service as a teacher. I continue my practice and make decisions from a place of empowerment that are in alignment with my mind, heart, and spirit. I have learned much about trauma and the destructive impact it can have on our lives. We are not our trauma. We are so much more.

My vision with this book was to share a journey of healing around relationships and financial challenges and continue doing work I love. I take it one day at a time, one step at a time in a place of trust, grounded in love and grace.

My empowering mantra is to fulfill my destiny by creating prosperity with grace and ease. I thank you for sharing my journey. May it inspire healing in you.

Namaste

Janet

About the Author

Prosperous Woman Coach Janet Kendrick honors every individual's birthright to experience happier, healthier lives and share their unique gifts and talents. Growing up in an unstable environment, a desire for happiness, healthy relationships, and financial freedom helped Janet heal by going inward, learning to trust her intuition, love herself, and helping others do the same. For her, a Prosperous Woman is expanding and growing in alignment with the highest version of herself by embracing harmony in life. She teaches tools that change from the inside out. With reverence, Janet shares the benefits of yoga, chakras, and the power of sacred money archetypes to help *create alignment in a misaligned world*. Her conviction that *our energy is our currency* is life-altering. She guides us in becoming conscious of and realigning our patterns and beliefs, and recognizing limitations that hold us back. This work enables living authentic, enriching lives.

Instagram | Facebook | LinkedIn
www.janetkendrick.com
Have you discovered your sacred money archetype?

Additional Resources

Our healing journeys are unique, and the paths I was led to may not resonate with you. However, there are so many resources to support healing. I encourage you to keep exploring, as the road is not always easy, and we don't have to go it alone. I want to provide tools that may help you on your journey. First, trust your intuition; if you ask for help, be open to receiving the answer, trust when you receive it, and take action. I lived in unhealthy relationships and experienced relationship violence that caused trauma for me. I was unaware because it was normal. Awareness is critical to change, and violence in relationships or unhealthy patterns are issues that we are capable of changing. We are worthy of having happier lives, healthy relationships, and a sense of safety to grow in who we are.

- Embracing the tools that came into my life moved me from a place of denial to creating the reality I desired. You will find several resources listed in this book and on my website. www.janetkendrick.com

- Jacqueline Aitken Executive Director and Heather King, Program Manager/group facilitator at Pace Community Support, Sexual Assault, and Trauma Centre, Grande Prairie, AB. Graciously agreed to let me share an assessment that is included in a training for intimate partner violence to help women identify patterns of abuse and where the person offending may need help.

- Adverse Childhood Experiences (ACES) is a resource to help identify the impacts of abuse at an early age that can impact mental and physical health in adulthood.

- The Sacred Money Archetypes assessment is a money personality quiz that helps you identify your patterns, gifts, strengths, and motivations regarding money.

www.ingramcontent.com/pod-product-compliance
Lightning Source LLC
Chambersburg PA
CBHW030434010526
44118CB00011B/636